VEGETARIAN
················ *to* ·······················

VEGAN

GIVE UP DAIRY. GIVE UP EGGS.
FOR GOOD.

sarah taylor
recipes by Mark Reinfeld

Published by:
The Vegan Next Door
14 Point Fosdick Dr NW
Gig Harbor, WA 98335
www.TheVeganNextDoor.com

Printed in the the United States of America

ISBN: 978-0-9764414-2-7

For every person who
cares enough to change.

Vegetarian to Vegan Success Stories

"Studying spirituality led me to become vegetarian....Then last year, after 3 years of being vegetarian, a friend pointed out the inconsistencies in my reasoning for being vegetarian. She said if I really cared about animals and didn't want to be contradictory, then I would be vegan. This five-minute conversation turned it all around for me. I became vegan on the spot and continue to be nine months later. I feel more aligned with my spiritual path, acknowledging my morals and ethics every time and sit down to eat a meal. Vegan for life!"
– Jahan Khamsehzadeh (age 28) Oakland, CA

"Much to my regret I was 35 before becoming vegetarian. To my even greater regret it took another 10 years before I had the sense to become vegan, whereupon the hay fever from which I'd suffered badly for 20 years disappeared.... I can continue to spend time outdoors in the late spring and summer with nary the slightest tickle in the throat, never mind the feeling that there was a red-hot carving knife in it, the itchy weepy eyes, the streaming nose and constant sneezing."
– Patricia Tricker, Bedale, UK

"I was nervous before I went vegan – what if I said I was going to go vegan but I couldn't stick to it? I was worried – I even had nightmares! Then I decided I simply had to be vegan – I had to cut out the animal cruelty that still comes with being vegetarian. I have been vegan for about 10 years now and have never looked back."
– Karin Ridgers, Essex, UK

"I turned from vegetarian to vegan after the birth of my son. I got mastitis when nursing and was in agony. I looked it up on the web and found out that a lot of cows get it and are not treated. I then read more and realized that while I was allowed to be a mother, the animals we use for milk are usually not. I have now been a vegan for 5 years."
– Jill Phillips, Cheshire, UK

"I was vegetarian for about 15 years, and making the move to being a vegan made great sense. I love animals, and felt bad about forcing a cow, sheep or goat to have babies just so we humans could have their milk for our babies ... and taking eggs felt wrong. My health has also improved and I have more energy. I love all the delicious vegan food you can have nowadays – there really is no reason not to be one. Healthy, sustainable and compassionate."
– Sue Andrew, North Wales, UK

"Going vegan was the best thing I ever did.... My only regret is that I didn't do it earlier. How many animals' lives could I have saved if I had? Every day, every meal is a joy because I know I'm doing no harm. It's peace of mind but it's also incredible food."
– Sue Henderson, Manchester, UK

"I was born in 1935 – four years before the start of the second world war. When I was fourteen years of age I gave up meat because I simply couldn't stomach the stuff. In 1962 I became a vegan and for most of my life I have enjoyed good health.... It has never been easier to be a complete vegetarian."
– George Barwick, Swansea, UK

CONTENTS

ACKNOWLEDGMENTS

With great joy and gratitude, I thank my husband, Mark Taylor. You inspire me and support me, always cheering me on and believing in me. Life with you is most definitely a symbiotic love affair!

For lovingly and tirelessly guiding me onto my path, I'd like to thank my parents, George and Virginia Kenefick. Your sacrifices are more appreciated than I can ever relay, and I love you tremendously.

With deep appreciation, I thank the very talented Mark Reinfeld. Your incredible recipes make going vegan truly delicious ... and you are a dream to work with!

For their unending support and encouragement, I'd like to thank my family and friends: Karen Kenefick-Massand, Ruth Arnold, Charlotte Cavoores, Carol Schaeffer, Sharon Galbraith, Emily Boller, Kamelia Enzler, Laurelee Blanchard, Barry Sultanoff and Meenakshe Angel Honig. I am so blessed to be surrounded by so much love.

For their willing assistance with stories, photos and medical references, I'd like to thank Laurelee Blanchard, Founder of Leilani Farm Sanctuary, Mercy for Animals, JoAnne MacArthur, PETA, Steve Blake, ScD and Bill Harris, MD.

For their help in creating this book, I thank editor Virginia Kenefick, graphics designer Robyn Rolfes at Creative Syndicate, typesetters Jim and Barbara Weems at AdGraphics and printer Melody Morris at Sun Graphics.

With great respect I thank John Robbins, whose book, *Diet for a New America*, not only turned me vegan overnight, but also set me on a spiritual trajectory that has changed my life forever. I also thank Neal Barnard, MD, President of the Physician's Committee for Responsible Medicine, for writing the foreword for my book, and for fighting the hardest battles of all for the animals – those in Washington DC.

Finally, here's to all the vegetarians who strive to become vegan. I commend you for setting your intentions on being 100% vegan, and my deepest desire in writing this book is to help you get there!

FOREWORD

You've heard about it. It is what Bill Clinton used to trim his waistline and restore his heart health. It powered Serena Williams to victories at Wimbledon, the U.S. Open, and the Olympics. A plant-based [vegan] diet helps celebrities, athletes, and millions of other people to be their very best.

People who put vegan foods to work have knocked out chronic aches and pains, gotten off their medications, boosted their energy, and even revitalized their sex lives. And yes, they are the slimmest, healthiest people on the block.

In our research studies at the Physicians Committee for Responsible Medicine, we have seen so many people who had tried countless other approaches to health, only to end in frustration. Once they begin to take advantage of the power of a smartly planned plant-based diet, everything finally turns around.

Yes, you might be thinking, that vegan landscape looks like a great place to be, but how do I get there? It might not sound so easy. To get to a healthy diet, you'll have to cross through a torrent of questions and challenges. At least that's the way it might seem at first glance.

Well, if that's the way you're feeling, relax. In *Vegetarian to Vegan*, Sarah Taylor shows you the stepping stones that will make your journey easy. As she will show you, it is easier than you had ever imagined.

First, you'll get the facts you need about why a change makes so much sense. If you have already broken away from meat, but are continuing a love affair with cheddar cheese or eggs Benedict, you'll learn why taking a few additional steps will pay off all the way around—for you, the animals, and the environment. Or if healthy eating in general is new for you, you'll get all the basic information you need. And then, you'll be able to focus on the how—how to make it work in your life, whether you're at home, at a restaurant, or on the road. It is easier than you had ever imagined. You'll know all the best choices and will find a treasure trove of delicious recipes and menu ideas.

Whether you decide to use your healthy new menu to power an athletic career or a high-profile life in the public eye, or you simply want to look good and feel great, you will be so glad you made this important step. And you'll inspire others to do the same.

Neal D. Barnard, MD
President, Physicians Committee
for Responsible Medicine
Washington, DC

INTRODUCTION

People for the Ethical Treatment of Animals (PETA) says that vegetarians save the lives of 100 land animals each and every year. Vegetarians also help our environment by not supporting the meat industry, which has a terrible impact on our air, water and soil. Of course, they are also doing something very good for their health in the process, as the vegetarian diet has consistently been shown to be associated with lower rates of heart disease, diabetes and cancer, among other illnesses, and vegetarians, on average, are much trimmer than their fellow omnivorous humans.

Yet with all that success, there are still some major challenges with the vegetarian diet: Although vegetarians help millions of animals in the meat industry avoid a brutal slaughter, billions more animals in the dairy and egg industries are forced to live horrifying lives … only to be slaughtered alongside their brothers and sisters from the meat industry in the exact same slaughterhouses at the end of their painful lives.

Additionally, while the livestock industry in general is a major cause of environmental damage, the dairy and egg industries are often considered worse than the meat industry in many of the leading environmental indicators. In fact, the dairy industry has been targeted as one of the most environmentally damaging industries in the world.

Furthermore, many leading physicians and nutritionists are now calling dairy products "liquid meat" due to their terrible effects on our health. Almost all dairy products are full of saturated fat and cholesterol, and have been linked to heart disease, diabetes, osteoporosis, autoimmune diseases and many cancers. Even fat-free dairy products are linked to many of these same problems, as we'll discuss. And while vegetarians are generally healthier than their meat-eating friends and family members, many are still overweight from eating high-fat dairy products and eggs, and can suffer from all the same health issues as meat-eaters.

So, while the vegetarian diet offers incredible benefits over the standard meat and dairy based diet, it doesn't touch the suffering of the billions of animals in the dairy and egg industries, is still extremely taxing on the environment and can sabotage an otherwise healthy diet.

The vegan diet can resolve all of those problems. A healthy vegan diet confers no harm on animals, minimal impact on the environment, and is considered by many physicians and nutritionists to be the optimal diet for human health.

Yet, while countless vegetarians have a strong desire to go vegan, many are simply overwhelmed by the thought. People often lament, "I've been vegetarian for years, but I just can't seem to give up dairy!" In fact, hundreds of vegetarians complain that, as hard as they try, they just can't find a way to give up some favorite vegetarian food that is not vegan. Most often it is cheese or chocolate, or perhaps it is baked goods that contain eggs. In fact, it can seem downright masochistic to give up more food groups when it seems like you've already given up so much to become vegetarian!

If this sounds like you, I want you to know that I really understand. When I give a speech, I always tell my audiences that, before I went vegan, my four food groups were Swiss, Havarti, Cheddar and Chocolate – and I mean it! As soon as I went to college (and thus began making my own food choices), I gravitated to all things dairy – melted cheese hoagies, grilled cheese sandwiches, macaroni & cheese and frozen yogurt with M&Ms on top. I also adored baked goods, which almost always contain eggs and butter. So trust me … I *know* what it's like to love dairy and egg products!

Yet there are thousands of vegans who have found a way to give all that up and truly never miss it. I am one of them. The tipping point that makes you go vegan once and for all may come when you finally understand just how bad dairy products are for your health, when you hear a statistic about the environmental impact of dairy and egg farming, or see a graphic photo about the cruelty that happens in dairy and egg farms – yes, even "cage free" and "organic" farms.

You may be thinking, "But I've read all that information and none of it has convinced me to go vegan! I have even tried going vegan for a while, but I just couldn't stick with it." If that is the case, then let me assure you – you either haven't come across the right information yet, or you simply weren't ready to receive it ... and there is nothing as powerful as coming across the right piece of information at the right time. When you finally come across that compelling book, photo, statistic, or video at the right time in your life, you will likely find that you do not need motivation or willpower to give up dairy – it will just become something you do effortlessly. So don't feel like you're a hopeless cause if you saw horrible photos of the dairy industry and still couldn't get yourself to change ... it simply wasn't compelling enough information for you, or it didn't come at the right time.

I'm hoping that now, as you read this book, it is your time – your time to finally receive the information in a way that will move you to make the ultimate change to a vegan diet; your time to stop the cycle of trying and quitting; your time to stop wishing you were vegan ... and finally become one.

This book was written specifically to give you the motivation you need, combined with practical tools and delicious recipes to help you become fully vegan. Whether it happens overnight or over the course of some days or months, you *will* go vegan if that's your intent.

Welcome! I'm glad you're here, and I'm honored you have chosen this book.

Sarah Taylor
Gig Harbor, Washington
October 2013

"It's not that some people
have willpower and some don't.
It's that some people are ready
to change and others are not."
– James Gordon, MD

PART 1

Vegetarian to Vegan: WHY?

To make the change from a vegetarian to a vegan diet, you will need two things: A strong enough reason to do it, and the tools to help you succeed.

The goal of Part 1 in this book is to give you a strong enough reason to give up dairy and egg products forever. In fact, this book – presumably because it focuses solely on information *specific to the dairy and egg industries* – uncovers an incredible amount of information that has not been discussed before in other vegan books. Although you may think you've "heard it all before" when it comes to veganism, you are very likely to find a lot of new information in this section that you actually haven't come across before.

To convince you to give up dairy and eggs, Part 1 needs to be extremely compelling. We will start with a topic that may be uncomfortable, but is certainly compelling: How dairy cows and egg-laying hens are living in our country's factory farms. Most readers will probably make up their mind to give up dairy and eggs after these first two chapters. But don't worry – if you need even more motivation to make the commitment, the chapters on the effects that dairy and egg products have on your health and on our environment follow. By the end of Part 1, you should have all the motivation you need to finally declare yourself a vegan … for good. Let's begin.

"The animals of the world
exist for their own reasons.
They were not made for humans
any more than blacks were made
for whites, or women for men."
– Alice Walker

Chapter 1
DAIRY FARMS

The dairy industry is big business. In fact, if you look at the industry solely from a business standpoint, they have had remarkable success. Between 1950-2000, the industry has been able to decrease the number of cows in the U.S. by over 50% (from about 22 million to 9.2 million cows) yet they have managed to more than triple their output per cow (from 5,314 pounds of milk to 18,204 pounds) for an overall increase in production using half the number of cows![1] From a business standpoint, this is a huge success in productivity.

Yet, we have to remember that cows are not machines – they are sentient beings who do feel pain and have emotions. Most things come at a cost, and in the case of the dairy industry's incredible business success, the cows pay heavily. Tripling a cow's natural production rate involves genetically and pharmaceutically manipulating the cow to produce much more milk than nature intended, and this has a multitude of side effects, as we'll see in the coming chapter.

If you have ever wondered what's wrong with consuming dairy products since the cows are not slaughtered to get their milk, then this chapter is for you.

COWS

In nature, cows are very peaceful creatures. They are not naturally aggressive, and they generally get along well with each other. They graze in pastures or grassy lands, and raise their young with their herd. Animal behaviorists have found that cows have a complex hierarchy within their herds, and choose leaders based on intelligence, inquisitiveness, confidence, experience and good social skills rather than simply based on size, force or aggression.[2] They develop very strong bonds between mother and calf, and form cliques within their herds. In fact, they are even known to hold grudges against other cows and humans that treat them poorly!

Cows are intelligent, too. According to the Humane Society of the United States, cows learn from each other: If one cow gets shocked by an electric fence, the others in the herd will learn from it and stay back from the fence.

Interestingly, cows are also very emotionally sensitive: Researchers at Purdue University found that cows produced significantly more milk when spoken to gently than when they were shouted at and handled roughly, and mishandled cows give less milk, particularly when the person who mishandles them is present at milking.[3] In another study, cows' heart rates increased when they listened to an audio recording of people yelling versus an equally loud recording of metal clanging[4]; cows appear to get stressed or scared when they know people are mad.

Cows can be quite affectionate towards humans, and have been known to "cuddle" and rub up against their favorite people, "talk" to them, and follow them around while they do farm chores.

They can live quite healthfully for 13-20 years with few or no medical issues if given enough shelter, water, and land to roam and graze.

FACTORY FARMS

Sadly, the vast majority of these gentle cows in our dairy system live a very different kind of life from the grassy pastureland that many people imagine. The dairy industry would like us to believe that our milk and dairy products come from happy cows grazing peacefully on rolling hills, but nothing could be further from the truth.

Crowding and Indoor Living

Almost all the dairy cows in the United States and other industrialized countries live in factory farms, with few exceptions. As the name implies, factory farms are farms that have been turned into huge factories, and house up to fifteen thousand[5] cows per building. Instead of providing ample land for cows to roam and graze, cows are packed into huge warehouses, each given a small stall that barely gives her room to move around. Air quality becomes toxic and the conditions very unsanitary when so many animals live in the same building. Most of the farm processes – like feeding, watering, and milking – are automated to reduce the need for large numbers of employees. This system allows the "farmers" to maximize production and profits.

Cows Crowded in a Dairy Farm
Incredibly close quarters in factory farms help
disease to spread quickly amongst animals.
Photo Courtesy of Mercy for Animals

While we'd all like to believe that dairy cows have plenty of room to roam and graze on rolling, grassy hills, the reality is that most dairy cows will rarely, if ever, get to breathe fresh air from the outdoors, feel the sun on their backs, the wind in their hair or rain drops from above. They will literally live their lives inside a very small stall, under artificial lighting, standing in their own urine and feces, fighting off bacterial infections, viruses, and respiratory illnesses that result from living in the waste and inhaling the toxic fumes that thousands of crowded cows create.

Milking

Dairy cows in a factory farm are forced to work very hard to provide consumers with milk for their dairy products. They are hooked up to electric milking machines several times each day. These milking machines enable a single farm worker to milk more than eighty-five cows in two hours. These machines often cause cuts and injuries, and in some cases can give cows repeated electric shocks. The vacuum pressure applied to the teats also is a major cause for a disease called mastitis, which we will discuss later.

Dehorning

Dairy cows are usually born with horn tissue that, if left alone, will grow into horns. Farmers, however, generally cut off this sensitive horn tissue to keep the dairy workers and other cows safe from goring. This practice is called "dehorning."

Dehorning is generally performed by slicing off the tissue or horn with a searing hot blade. However, some dairy farmers use handsaws, blades or chemicals to take the horns off. Sadly, because anesthesia is expensive, it is almost never used. The cows often thrash around in pain and struggle violently, so they have to be restrained during the dehorning process. According to Temple Grandin, noted Animal Behaviorist and Professor of Animal Science at Colorado State University, dehorning dairy cows is the single most painful procedure they have to go through.[6]

Like receiving electric shocks from milking machines or standing in urine and feces all day, dehorning is another example of a consequence that is unique to factory farms – it would never happen spontaneously in nature. Sadly, it can lead to hemorrhage, bone fractures, tissue necrosis, infection and even death.

Artificial Insemination

To keep productivity levels high, adult dairy cows on a factory farm are essentially expected to give milk at all times. Many people have never thought about what has to happen for a cow to constantly make milk: To make milk, a cow – just like a human – must be pregnant or nursing.

Therefore, a dairy cow is artificially inseminated over and over again, so that her entire adult life is one of being pregnant and giving birth. A dairy cow will spend over 300 days each year in milk production, and will be slaughtered after just four years, usually due to infection, disease or other health problems caused by her living conditions.

Separation

On a factory farm, cow's milk is not intended for baby cows – it's intended for humans. Therefore, baby calves are not allowed to nurse. They are taken from their mothers as soon as two hours after birth, and are either fed a commercial milk replacer that is made from dried milk powder, or they are fed milk that has been deemed unfit for human consumption.

Besides keeping the milk for humans to consume, there is another reason why baby calves in a factory farm are taken from their mothers so quickly: According to the Journal of Dairy Science,

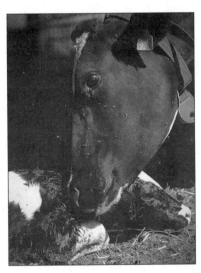

Newborn calf
A rare moment in a factory farm when a mother cow is able to nuzzle her newborn before it is quickly taken away from her.
Photo courtesy of JoAnne MacArthur, 2012

"Calves left with cows for more than two hours [of birth] had a higher risk for infection, possibly due to exposure to large amounts of infectious agents in the maternity pen."[7] Letting the calf stay with its mother for any significant period of time increases risk for Cryptosporidium infection[8] and respiratory disease, which increases calves' risk of death by six times.[9] Basically, these authors are saying that the "maternity wards" at the dairy factories are so filthy that the calves' lives are at risk if they hang around for more than a couple of hours.

Sadly, just like human mothers bond tightly with their newborn babies, so do cows bond with their calves. Mother cows have been reported to bellow for many hours or even days after her calf is taken from her. Author Oliver Sacks, MD discusses a visit that he and Temple Grandin made to a dairy farm: When they arrived, they heard many cows bellowing, causing a very loud and unnerving sound. Temple commented, "They must have separated the calves from the cows this morning," and indeed, that was exactly the case.[10] Similarly, John Avizienius, a senior scientific officer at the Farm Animal Department at the RSPCA in Britain, discusses one particular cow that suffered great emotional distress over the separation from her calf: She bellowed for hours, and even after six weeks would hover at the pen door where she had last seen her calf.[11]

In a cruel twist of fate, it's been shown in mammals that multiparous females (those giving birth for the second time or more) have higher levels of oxytocin than primiparous females (those giving birth for the first time.)[12] This means that with each subsequent birth, a mother cow presumably grows more and more bonded to her calves, and it likely becomes more and more emotionally traumatizing for the cow each time a baby calf is taken from her.

Just as the mother forms an immediate bond with her calf, the newborn calf also has an immediate attachment to his mother, and is healthier the longer he gets to bond with her. Calves allowed to remain with their mothers for up to 14 days showed weight gains at three times the rate of calves taken within 1-2 days, and they also showed signs of better searching behaviors and better social relationships with other calves.[13] But as we've seen, baby calves are taken away within hours due to both the risk of infection from their filthy conditions, as well as the desire for the farmers to keep the mother's milk for humans – not calves – so they can make a profit.

It has been shown that baby calves experience emotional distress when they are separated from their mothers. Unbelievably, they have been known to try to bond with the factory farm workers, even

The Sacred Cow

Photo courtesy of Laurelee Blanchard

Indians believe that the cow is a symbol of peace, and cows are therefore respected as sacred animals. They are not supposed to be slaughtered or harmed, and are permitted to roam the streets undisturbed. Gandhi has been quoted as saying, "The cow is a poem of compassion."

Many Indians hold a tradition called go-raksa and go seva where they give their first piece of bread at mealtime to a cow, and the second piece is kept as an offering to God – the cow is honored before God!

trying to suckle the fingers of the worker who is sending them off to slaughter.

Female calves will be raised to become dairy cows like their mothers, and the male calves will go to veal farms where they will be slaughtered for their tender meat.

DISEASES AND COMPLICATIONS OF LIVING ON A DAIRY FACTORY FARM

As we've discussed, dairy cows live in very unnatural, crowded and filthy conditions. They are not given sufficient room to move around, exercise or socialize, and are often never allowed to go outside. They are squeezed into buildings with thousands of other cows, where diseases and viruses spread quickly. They are also hooked up to automated milking machines several times a day that can wreak havoc with their bodies. These conditions create a multitude of problems for the cows that they generally wouldn't face in natural conditions,

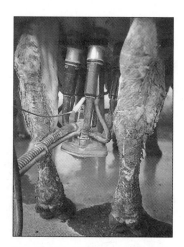

Electric milking machine

Cows in factory farms are not milked by hand; instead, they are hooked up to mechanized milking machines several times a day. Notice the wet floor that is so harmful to their hooves, and how filthy her legs are from the factory farm conditions.

Photo courtesy of JoAnne MacArthur, 2012

such as mastitis, milk fever, Bovine Immunodeficiency Virus, Bovine Leukemia Virus, paratuberculosis, Mad Cow Disease, endometritis and lameness.

Mastitis

Dairy cows on a factory farm are not milked by hand, as in years past. Instead, they are hooked up to automated milking machines several times a day, and the machines squeeze the milk out of the cows' teats. This mechanized process can cause many problems, including cuts, injuries, electric shock and infection. The most common condition that arises from mechanized milking machines is an infection of the udders called mastitis. Mastitis is a potentially fatal infection of the mammary glands that can be incredibly painful, and is a major cause of early slaughter.

Cows have two natural defense mechanisms to help them avoid mastitis: The first way that cows ward off mastitis is through sphincter muscles in the teat that close when the cow is not being milked. These muscles close off the teat so that bacteria cannot make their

Mastitis
A dairy cow suffers from the very painful condition of mastitis.
Notice the telltale swollen udder from the infection.

way up into the mammary glands. The second way that cows naturally ward off mastitis is through the lining of the teat canal, which helps to protect the teat canal and keep bacteria from moving up it.

However, today's mass-milking procedures degrade a cow's teats by applying excess vacuum pressure to them, which results in calloused and distended teats. Scar tissue forms in the teat canal, which can make it difficult for milk to pass through the teat, causing milk to flow very slowly or not at all. These machines also degrade the sphincter muscles in the teats and damage the protective lining, making it easier for bacteria to move up the teats into the mammary glands. When bacteria infect mammary glands, this is the painful condition called mastitis.

Mastitis is a persistent, recurring problem that causes pus to appear in the cow's milk. While cows can be given antibiotics to treat the condition, their milk is not sellable until nearly all traces of the antibiotic are gone. Therefore, because high levels of both pus and drug residues are not acceptable in the final milk product, mastitis is a common reason that cows are sent to the slaughterhouse. The USDA estimates that approximately 43% of all factory farm dairy cows suffer from mastitis.[14]

Pus in Our Milk

While high levels of pus and antibiotics are not acceptable in the final milk product, U.S. regulations actually allow for some pus and antibiotics to be milk. The U.S. Federal and State Pasteurized Milk Ordinance decrees that the level of somatic cell counts (white blood cells that are pus) must not exceed 750,000 per milliliter.[15] One glass of milk, then, can have 180,000,000 puss cells and still be deemed acceptable for consumption. Reports show that there are usually still traces of both pus and antibiotic residues in milk samples.[16]

Milk Fever

Another condition found in dairy cows is Milk fever. Milk fever is a disease caused by low levels of calcium in the blood. Interestingly, the name "milk fever" is a bit misleading, as the cow's temperature will actually be lower than normal, not higher.

It takes a lot of calcium to produce milk, and as pointed out at the beginning of this chapter, dairy cows now make three times the amount of milk as they did in the 1950s. Since it takes so much calcium to produce milk, and cows are expected to make milk 300 days a year – far more than nature ever intended – the cow can develop low levels of calcium which can result in Milk fever. Milk fever is most common when a cow begins lactating; if she is using more calcium for milk production than her body is able to mobilize from her calcium reserves, she will have a net deficit of calcium in her blood, putting her at risk for milk fever.

Low blood calcium levels interfere with proper muscle function, which cause the cow to become weak. In mild cases of Milk Fever, a cow may have difficulty standing and may stagger or fall down. In more severe cases, the cow will lose her appetite and eventually go into heart failure.[17] She will lie on the ground, unable to rise.

Fortunately, this disease can usually be treated with calcium injections, and most cows will recover from milk fever. However, these injections put the cows in danger of "heart blockade," which can cause death.

Milk fever is yet another example of a condition found almost exclusively on factory farms, where cows are kept pregnant and lactating most of their lives, and are forced to produce far more milk than what is natural for their bodies.

Bovine Immunodeficiency Virus

Bovine Immunodeficiency Virus (BIV) is a retrovirus that is akin to HIV in humans, but affects cows. Like HIV, BIV is spread from cow to cow through bodily fluids. Because cows in factory farms are crowded together so closely, they are at a higher risk of transmitting

BIV than if they were living in natural conditions. When one animal in a herd tests positive, many others will usually also test positive. In the U.S., the rate of BIV prevalence is approximately 1-5%.[18]

While BIV doesn't always result in adverse clinical conditions for the cow, it can cause many noted symptoms such as encephalopathy (brain disease), decreased milk production, chronic ill health, and other problems from a lowered immune system, such as mastitis and other infections.

There are several ways that BIV is spread in factory farms. One is through reusing contaminated needles, as farmers try to save money and/or time on new needles. Another way BIV is spread is through communal sharing of colostrum by calves who are not allowed to suckle from their own mother's teats. Finally, failure to completely sterilize instruments after they have been used for invasive procedures is another method whereby BIV can be transmitted from one cow to another.[19] Once again, these are all situations that don't generally arise in natural conditions, and are predominantly found in factory farms.

Bovine Leukemia Virus

Bovine Leukemia Virus (BLV) is a viral infection that can spread throughout a herd of cows. Not all cows exposed to the virus will become infected. Of those infected, though, about 2-5% will develop tumors in their lymph nodes.[20] These cows will generally lose their appetite and get very thin, their milk production will drop and they can suffer from rear-limb weakness or paralysis, fever, protruding eyeballs, gastrointestinal obstruction, abnormal heartbeat and increased blood lymphocyte count. Significant mortality can occur in a herd, and there are no treatments for this condition.

BLV can spread via many different routes, including blood, colostrum, milk, in uterus, and possibly by large biting flies. In nature, nursing calves are the most susceptible to getting infected.

In today's modern factory farms, BLV spreads through a host of unnatural methods not found in nature. Artificial insemination,

Bovine Leukemia Virus
This cows enlarged lymph nodes on the side of the her
face and neck are telltale signs of Bovine Leukemia Virus.

gouge dehorning, vaccination, ear tagging, tattooing and rectal palpation are all ways where BLV can be transmitted between cows. In a 2007 study, approximately 84% of cows in U.S. dairy operations were positive for BLV.[21]

There is no treatment for BLV, and infected cows are condemned to death and their meat is not sellable. In California alone, about 5,200 cows per year are condemned due to BLV, and the numbers being condemned are three times higher than they were in the 1970s.[22]

Paratuberculosis (Johne's Disease)
Paratuberculosis, often called "Johne's Disease" after veterinarian Heinrich Johne who discovered it in 1905, is a bacterial infection of the small intestine. It is contagious, chronic and can be fatal.

Johne's Disease is problematic on dairy farms. The infection usually occurs in newborn calves who often swallow a small amount of infected manure in the birthing pen or on the mother's udder. As previously mentioned, the birthing pens in dairy farms are filthy, despite efforts to keep them clean, and Johne's Disease is one of the byproducts of filthy birthing pens.

In Johne's Disease, the infected tissues of the intestine begin to thicken as white blood cells congregate in an attempt to fight off the infection. This thickening of the intestines prevents nutrients from being absorbed (a primary role of intestines) and diarrhea, dehydration and cachexia (wasting) results. The animals become emaciated and often die.[23]

When a cow is infected with Johne's Disease she will often either eliminate the infection or become an asymptomatic carrier. However, if symptoms occur, the disease will progress and the cow will eventually die. One study of 121 dairy herds in Michigan found that 54% of herds tested positive for Johne's Disease, and 6.9% of the cows tested positive.[24]

Mad Cow Disease

Mad cow disease is officially called "bovine spongiform encephalopathy" (BSE) in cows, and "new variant Creutzfeldt-Jakob disease" (nvCJD) in humans. This disease occurs when prions enter the body, usually by ingesting the meat, blood, bones, or neural tissues of an infected animal. (Cooking the meat or tissue does not kill off the prions.) Prions are misfolded proteins that are infectious; when a prion enters the body, it will begin a deadly process of converting healthy proteins into diseased prions, causing a chain reaction of destruction. It generally takes about 8 months to 10 years for symptoms to develop.

Mad cow disease is characterized by brain degeneration, where the brain gets holes in it until it looks "spongy." Infection can result in memory loss, dementia, inability to communicate, convulsions, lack of coordination and balance, inability to stand, behavioral and personality changes, aggression, brain damage, and finally, death. All known prion diseases affect the brain or neural tissues, and are currently untreatable and fatal.[25]

In the United Kingdom, where mad cow disease has had it's worst effect, more than 180,000 cows have been infected, and 4.4 million cows have been slaughtered in an attempt to eradicate the disease.[26] The first case of mad cow disease in the U.S. was discovered in 1993, and the most recent case was in 2012.

Many people wonder how cows are getting Mad Cow Disease if they are herbivores and supposedly eating grass and grains – not the meat, bones, blood or neural tissue of other animals. In nature, cows eat grass, but in factory farms they are fed commercial feed. Commercial feeds are mostly made of grains or soybeans, but can also contain meat and bone meal, which comes from slaughterhouse left-overs and the cadavers of sick and injured animals. It's thought that the first case of mad cow came from a cow that ingested feed that came from infected sheep, so this disease passes from species to species, including, of course, to humans.

Due to the mad cow disease outbreak, it is now illegal in Japan and Europe to feed the bone, blood or discarded meat products to other animals in their feed; however, this practice is still allowed to some extent in the U.S. As of 1997 in the U.S., while cows cannot be fed the meat and bone meal of other mammals, other animals (like chickens) can, and their meat and bone meal can be turned around and fed back to cows! As mentioned, the most recent case of mad cow disease (BSE) in the U.S. was found in 2012, so it is not likely that these U.S. regulations are keeping mad cow disease at bay.

Additionally, while Japan and the European countries test every slaughtered cow for mad cow disease, the USDA only requires U.S. slaughterhouses to test less than 1% of slaughtered cows. Many people feel that these practices put U.S. citizens at risk of developing the disease.

Why is all of this relevant to vegetarians who don't eat meat? It's relevant because dairy cows are at the same risk as beef cows for getting this disease. As long as there is a demand for dairy products, dairy cows will be kept in factory farms and given feed that could put them at risk of developing this cruel and terrible disease.

Endometritis

Endometritis is a condition characterized by inflammation of the inner lining of the uterus, called the endometrium. It is another example of a type of infection which, as we've seen in dairy factories, can be very high due to the crowded and dirty conditions. Cows are most susceptible to getting endometritis during calving and the post-calving period, as the vaginal canal is susceptible to infection due to the trauma and lesions caused during the birthing process.

Endometritis can cause reduced reproductive performance, loss of appetite, decreased milk production and a pussy vaginal discharge.[27] In one study, endometritis was found in 53% of cows among herds in five New York commercial dairy farms.[28]

Treatment for endometritis is antibiotics. Some affected cows will have acute endometritis, meaning it is temporary and resolves quickly with treatment; other cows, however, will suffer from chronic endometritis, and continually battle this type of infection.

Once again, this condition is generally brought about by the unnatural conditions of the dairy factory farms. Since endometritis is associated with birthing and dairy cows are forced to give birth over and over to produce milk, this is a problem that is particularly high in dairy herds as opposed to herds raised for their meat. Furthermore, as mentioned before, the birthing pens are filthy, which is the main cause for infection. Prevention is taught by simple hygiene in calving facilities, with plenty of ventilation, sanitary conditions, and avoidance of overcrowding. Unfortunately, since prevalence rates among dairy cows hover around 53%, it doesn't appear that this advice is being followed very well.

Lameness

One of the most costly conditions for dairy farmers is lameness. A study of New York dairy herds estimated that there are approximately 30 cases of lameness per 100 cows a year, at a cost of $9,000/100 cows/year.[29] For a dairy that has 15,000 cows, lameness would cost $1,350,000 a year. On modern dairy farms, lameness ranges from 5% to 50%, depending on how well-managed the dairy farm is run.[30]

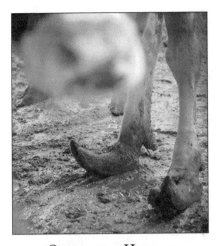

Overgrown Hooves

A cow with overgrown hooves standing
on a hard floor that is covered in muck.

Photo courtesy of JoAnne MacArthur, 2012

Ninety percent of lameness cases are due to foot problems, particularly of the rear feet, which bear most of a cow's weight.

One major problem that occurs with the feet is laminitis. Laminitis is characterized by an inflammation of the laminae, which is essentially the layer between the hoof wall and the bone. This problem primarily occurs from standing on hard floors all day, rather than on the soft ground that cows are designed to stand on.

Interdigital dermatitis, another condition that can lead to lameness, is characterized by inflammation of the interdigital skin. The skin begins to thicken due to the inflammation, becomes painful when touched, and smells putrid. According to a report from the Proceedings from the 2000 Kentucky Dairy Conference, "Interdigital dermatitis ... is believed to be associated with conditions that create a moist claw environment combined with exposure to manure and slurry."[31] Interdigital dermatitis is often followed by or associated with heel horn erosion.

Heel horn erosion is a condition affecting the bulb of the heel, and is also called "slurry heel" because it often occurs when animals are constantly standing in "slurry" – a mucky combination mainly made up of feces, urine and mud. The moist environment softens the heel horn, and the bacteria from the slurry get inside the softened horn, causing the heel horn to erode. According to the Merck Veterinary Manual, "The prevalence of heel horn erosion is highest during the winter, particularly when the claws are exposed to an unhygienic, moist environment (such as exists in intensively managed dairy units)."[32] Heel horn erosion doesn't cause lameness in every case, but if it advances far enough, it can result in lameness. When it advances, the cow starts to change her stance, pushing more weight on her front legs so they can absorb more of the shock.

The Demand for Dairy

The demand is high for dairy products, and since all dairy products begin as milk, milk producers have been diligently trying to find ways to squeeze more milk out of each cow.

Growing demand for cheese has been one of the biggest forces shaping the U.S. dairy industry. Per capita cheese use has risen to twice the level that it was twenty-five years ago. We may think that we're just sprinkling a little cheese on our burrito, or putting a little creamer in our coffee, but our dairy consumption adds up to a substantial amount per person.

To provide for our growing demand for cheese and other dairy products, genetic manipulation, bovine growth hormones and intensive production technologies have made it possible for modern dairy cows to produce a hundred pounds of milk a day – many times more than they would produce naturally.

A common condition that occurs from both laminitis and advanced heel horn erosion is sole ulcers, where ulcers occur in the soles of the foot. Sole ulcers are one of the most debilitating forms of lameness in dairy cows.

Foot rot is yet another health complication associated with factory farm conditions. Foot rot is a contagious disease that can spread amongst cattle. It appears as lesions in the interdigital skin that begin to rot as the skin dies. It produces a foul odor, and can turn into an infection that can eventually spread up the leg, causing almost certain lameness. According to a report from the Proceedings from the 2000 Kentucky Dairy Conference, "Environmental factors associated with these disorders may include housing conditions which require cows to walk through or stand in manure slurry for extended periods. Since the causative organisms are believed to originate from the gastrointestinal tract of the cow it would be reasonable to expect that manure management would be helpful to reducing the occurrence of the disease."[33]

Sadly, lameness and foot problems like laminitis, interdigital dermatitis, heel horn erosion, sole ulcers and foot rot are further examples of painful conditions that arise from unnatural and filthy living conditions created by massive dairy farms. One study concluded that "the risk factors of heelhorn erosion were associated with poor hygiene, while the risk factors of subacute laminitis were linked to uncomfortable housing conditions: high steps and slopes, and discomfort when lying down and getting up."[34] Yet again, these are all conditions that arise from keeping thousands of cows in an unnatural environment, putting them at severe risk of disease, and causing them pain and, often, an early death.

SLAUGHTER

A cow living in a natural setting will live between 13-20 years on average, but a dairy cow in a factory farm is slaughtered after less than 4 years.[35] The most prevalent reason that dairy cows go to slaughter is due to reproductive issues, and the second most common reason is due to mastitis.[36]

Sadly, 3% of dairy cows are so unhealthy that they are deemed unfit for human consumption, and their meat is never used. In 1999 the National Cattleman's Association did an audit where it found that of the dairy cows headed to slaughter 7% had arthritis, which results in about 40 pounds of meat being unusable per cow, and 88% of the cows had bruising that resulted in up to 15% of their meat being unsellable. (The bruising often came from rough handling during the slaughtering process.) About 1% of the cows still had antibiotic residues in their meat, making them unfit for consumption: gentamycin, penicillin, sulfadimethoxine, streptomycin and tetracyclines are all examples of antibiotics found in the dairy meat supply.[37] In 2009, approximately 19% of the U.S. beef supply came from dairy cows that had been sent to slaughter, usually due to reproductive problems or disease.[38]

Many well-meaning vegetarians don't eat meat because they know that the animals are brutally slaughtered for their meat. However, they can't understand what's ethically wrong with eating dairy products when the cows aren't slaughtered to provide us with milk.

What they don't realize – but you now do – is that these cows live an average of four long years in a state of constant pregnancy, having their babies torn from them within hours of birth, brutally dehorned, living inside a crowded and filthy building their whole lives generally without access to the outdoors, subjected to high rates of disease, hooked up to mechanized milking machines every day, and having a very high risk for developing one or more diseases, such as mastitis, milk fever, Bovine Immunodeficiency Virus, Bovine Leukemia Virus, paratuberculosis, Mad Cow Disease, endometritis and lameness.

And here is the kicker…

After living a miserable life in these horrible factories to get consumers the dairy products they so badly want, dairy cows then go to the exact same slaughterhouse that a beef cow goes.

Cows may be transported to the slaughterhouse in extreme cold or heat, depending on the time of year, and will be crowded into a truck or train in a dark compartment where they will likely stand in fear and extreme discomfort for hours or even days. Cows have been known to collapse in hot weather, or freeze to the inside walls of transportation trucks in cold weather, where upon they have to be pryed off the walls with crowbars. Due to sorely lacking animal transportation laws, they have little or no rights to water, food, space to lie down or protection from the weather for the entire trip, even if it takes many days.

Many cows, upon arrival, are too weak, sick or injured to stand or walk off the trucks. These cows are called "downers." Downed cows cannot be used for food, so these cows will often be beaten, prodded in their faces and even shocked in their rectums to get them to stand up and start walking. If the workers can successfully get a downed cow to walk just a few hundred feet to the slaughter line, they can save the cow from being labeled as "downed," and profit can be made. Downed cows are a large source of lost revenue, so workers are encouraged to beat and shock the sick and injured cows aggressively to avoid lost profits. Sadly, most cows – not just downer cows – are treated brutally on their way to slaughter: You may remember the statistic that 88% of cows have bruising that results in some of their meat not being sellable … this is where much of that bruising occurs – from being brutally mishandled on their way to slaughter.

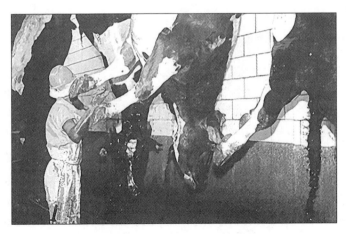

Cows on the slaughter line.

When a cow reaches the front of the slaughter line, she is supposed to be shot in the head with either an electric stun gun or a steel bolt to her brain, hopefully killing her quickly, or at least rendering her unconscious. However, both have problems: The high levels of electricity in the stun guns can cause the animals to jerk violently, putting the workers at risk for serious injury. Therefore, the workers often turn the electricity down to avoid injury to themselves. However, lowering the electricity increases the rate of unsuccessful stunning, and many cows are only partially stunned or not stunned at all when they head to the slaughter line ... where they are slaughtered fully conscious. Similarly, with the steel bolt guns, a worker can often miss the cow's brain, and because the line is moving fast, the worker is unable to try to stun her a second or third time. She, too, will head to the slaughter line alive and fully conscious.

In 2001, The Washington Post published an interview with a long-time slaughterhouse worker, Ramon Moreno. Here is an excerpt from the article:

> For 20 years, his post was "second-legger," a job that entails cutting hocks off carcasses as they whirl past at a rate of 309 an hour. The cattle were supposed to be dead before they got to Moreno. But too often they weren't:

> "They blink. They make noises," he said softly. "The head moves, the eyes are wide and looking around." Still Moreno would cut.

> On bad days, he says, dozens of animals reached his station clearly alive and conscious. Some would survive as far as the tail cutter, the belly ripper, the hide puller. "They die," said Moreno, "piece by piece."[39]

Videos from animal protection organizations show cows (and pigs) high in the air, dangling from their back hoof on the slaughter line, kicking and bellowing out in pain and fear. Nevertheless, they are sawed open from their neck to their groin fully conscious, as the meat extraction process begins. Not only is it ridiculously inhumane to slaughter these animals while they are still alive, but their kicking and thrashing are also additional serious causes of worker injury.

If you went vegetarian because these slaughterhouse conditions spoke so loudly to your sense of humanity that you decided you could never eat meat again, chew on this: Nearly all dairy cows will go to the exact same slaughter houses as the beef cows do – a total of 6.5 million dairy cows every single year[40] – and many of them are still alive as they go through it.

CONCLUSION

One reason people have a hard time giving up dairy products is because, unlike a big piece of steak where you can actually see the flesh and imagine the suffering that went into it, it's hard to make that same connection when you put a little cream in your milk or top your burrito with cheese.

Because dairy products don't visually remind us of the suffering that went into the product, it's easy to minimize your contribution to the cows' suffering. "It's only a tablespoon of creamer!" many people justify, or "It's only a bit of grated cheese!" It's difficult to understand that your tablespoon of creamer and your little bit of cheese, when added to all the other dairy products that you likely eat throughout the course of a given year, actually add up to a huge quantity. Quarts and quarts of milk, packages and packages of cheese, pints and pints of ice cream and yogurt – if most people had all their dairy products for a year laid out on your kitchen floor, they probably wouldn't be able to see the floor.

Now that you understand exactly how a dairy cow in a factory farm lives out her days – constantly pregnant, having her newborn calves torn from her just hours from birth, suffering a cruel dehorning process, living without access to sunshine, in steel cages with concrete floors under artificial lighting, eating mass produced grain instead of fresh grass, constantly fighting off illnesses and infections, all of which will shorten her lifespan by about 75% – well, hopefully it's become much easier to make that connection. As you finish this chapter, you can choose to eradicate any impact your diet has on cows suffering in factory farms by making the vow to eliminate dairy products from your diet.

What about Goat Dairies?

Goats on commercial dairy farms are typically regarded as commodities and depending on the level of care provided, can suffer from both physical and psychological disorders as goat dairy farms seek to maximize productivity and profitability. It is not uncommon for dairy goats on poorly managed farms to lack adequate veterinary care, suitable housing, or proper pasture. Due to the strong lobbying efforts of agribusiness, goats and all animals used for meat and dairy production are excluded from most state anti-cruelty laws and from the federal Animal Welfare Act.

A standard industry practice is to dehorn dairy goats before they are ten days old. A very hot iron is used to burn the horn buds off their heads. Dehorning is not only painful and traumatic for the goat, it's dangerous: The kid's brain can be permanently damaged by misuse of the disbudding iron. Infection and tetanus can also result from a botched dehorning job.

Like dairy cows, female goats on dairy farms are kept in a nearly constant state of pregnancy. They are typically impregnated while confined in a small pen with an aggressive buck. After the doe gives birth, her kids are taken away from her and the milk she produces is used for human consumption. The male offspring are sold for meat.

Ned the Dairy Goat, Saved from Slaughter

One February morning on the island of Maui, Bill, a friend of Leilani Farm Sanctuary, went for groceries at the market. When Bill heard crying coming from inside a car, he looked in the back seat and saw a goat tied up and in extreme distress. The car doors were locked, so Bill frantically waited, making eye contact with the goat until three men approached.

The men explained that they had just purchased the goat from a dairy farm and planned to butcher him that weekend for a barbeque. Bill pleaded with the men to relinquish the goat, but they refused. Unable to walk away, knowing the fate that awaited the goat, Bill decided there was no acceptable option other than buying the goat from the men.

Ned
Photo courtesy of Laurelee Blanchard, 2012

Bill named the goat Ned and brought him to Leilani Farm Sanctuary where he has been living for the past seven years. Ned, a sweet and gentle soul, seems to have forgotten his ordeal. He and his goat friends spend their days lounging under fruit trees in an orchard, grazing on lush grass in the pasture, and interacting with humans who give them endless love.

"The time will come when
men such as I will look upon the
murder of animals as they now
look upon the murder of men."
– Leonardo do Vinci

Chapter 2
EGG FARMS

Many vegetarians have read about the cruel conditions that broiler chickens (chickens raised for their meat) are kept in at the factory farms. However, they often don't know anything about the conditions that egg-laying hens live in. Many vegetarians wonder, "What wrong with eating eggs? We're not killing the chickens for their eggs, so what's wrong with eating them – especially if they are organic, cage-free, free-range eggs?" This is a great question, but if you like eating your eggs, you may not like the answer.

BROILER CHICKENS AND LAYING HENS

Chickens raised for meat are called "broiler chickens." They are genetically bred to grow very big, very fast so that the farmers can slaughter them early and get a lot of meat from each chicken. Laying hens – the chickens that supply consumers with eggs – are bred much differently. Because their purpose is to produce as many eggs as possible – not provide us with meat – they are bred to be much smaller in size, but prolific egg-makers.

There are more than 50 billion chickens produced each year for their meat and eggs.[41] While a hen a in a natural setting will live for about 6 years, a hen in a factory farm will be slaughtered after just 1 year; after producing approximately 300 eggs/year, her body is just too worn down to continue.[42]

BATTERY CAGES

Laying hens in most commercial egg farms are housed in cages called "battery cages." These cages are contained in a warehouse-like building, and are stacked in long rows on top of each other to maximize space. One building can literally hold hundreds of thousands of hens.

Each cage holds many hens, and is designed with a sloping floor so that when one of the hens lays an egg, the egg rolls to the edge of the cage where it drops into a gutter out of the hens' reach where it can be collected. Feeding and watering is usually automated, so human oversight of the birds is minimized and costs are reduced.

Battery cages are made of wire, including the floor. Because the cages are stacked on top of each other, when a bird urinates or defecates, that waste falls through the wire floor onto the birds below it. Under the bottom row of cages, there is a vast urine and feces pit. Because chicken feces is particularly high in ammonia, the stench in egg farms is incredibly overpowering.

Sadly, birds sometimes fall out of cages, get stuck between cages, or get their heads or limbs stuck between the bars of their cages. Because human oversight is so low, the birds are often not rescued, and die because they cannot access food and water.

Hens in Battery Cages
To maximize the use of the square footage in the warehouse,
hens are placed in battery cages that are stacked on top of each other. Each
hen has less room than a piece of paper in which to live for her entire life.
Photo Courtesy of Mercy for Animals

Battery cages, while outlawed in the European Union, are perfectly legal in the United States. About 75% of all commercial layer hens in the world and 95% in the United States are kept in battery cages.[43]

Legislation

In the European Union, battery cages were banned as of 2012, to be replaced with "enriched cages." Enriched cages will allow for more room (750 cm² versus ~ 500 cm²), a nest-box, litter, perches and claw shortening devices. While this is a step in the right direction, enriched cages are still very small, and are still nothing like a chicken's natural environment.

In the United States, there are very few laws that provide farm animals with any protection. Only a very small number of states have passed any laws to reduce the suffering associated with battery cages. The current recommendation by the United Egg Producers is 67 to 86 in² (430 to 560 cm²) per bird[44] – less than a sheet of paper.

COMPLICATIONS OF LIVING ON AN EGG FACTORY FARM

Crowding

Battery cages are about the size of a filing drawer, and each cage holds 8-10 hens. Each hen is given less room than the size of a sheet of paper. One hen needs about 32" to stretch her wings straight out, but with so many hens in such a small area, not one of them is able to stretch her wings. A hen in a battery cage will never be able to spread her wings her entire life.

Crowding in Battery Cages

In battery cages, many hens die when their necks, wings or feet get caught in the cage bars or wire floors. This hen's neck is stuck in the cage bars.

Photo Courtesy of Mercy for Animals

In addition to being cruel, this type of crowding causes many problems, such as high rates of infection and disease, foot and leg problems, as well as a condition called cage layer osteoporosis. Yet the worst problems arguably result from the psychological distress that the hens endure as they are not able to exhibit their natural behavior: They cannot walk more than a step or two, flap their wings, dustbathe, forage, perch, or nest, and of course, they have no access to natural light or the elements. Animal welfare scientists believe that these conditions are so unnatural for chickens that they result in the hens suffering from extreme frustration and boredom,[45] along with severe psychological problems. This can lead to a wide range of abnormal behaviors, including feather pecking, feather plucking, toe pecking, vent pecking, stereotype, polydipsia, cannibalism, and sham (or "vacuum") dustbathing.

ABNORMAL MEDICAL PROBLEMS DUE TO CROWDING

Infection

A battery cage – including the floor – is made of wire. Because the cages are stacked on top of each other, the hens' excrement drops through the wire floors onto the hens in the cages below them. The hens are thus covered in feces and urine, increasing their rate for illness.

In addition, the extreme crowding of the birds makes it very likely that if one hen gets sick it will pass the illness on to many others hens. This environment becomes a breeding ground for bacteria, and many hens suffer from illness and infection.

Filthy Conditions of Battery Cages

In factory farms, battery cages are stacked on top of each other to maximize square footage. Because they have wire floors, feces and urine fall from birds in the higher cages down to birds in the lower cages. Hens on a factory farm are generally covered in feces and urine.

Photo Courtesy of Mercy for Animals

Salmonella and e-Coli are rampant in egg laying facilities. Salmonella is three times higher in caged hens than in free-range hens.[46] The USDA found that e-coli is found in 99% of uncooked chicken meat.[47] Staphylococcus aureus, clostridium perfringens, campylobacter and listeria are all prevalent – often in high amounts – in chickens in the food industry. It is thought that these are some of the major causes of food-borne illnesses, and why consumers are cautioned to always cook their meat thoroughly.

Feet Problems

Because battery cages are so cramped, some hens won't be able to move around at all. Animal welfare workers have found that some hens stand in the same place for so many days on end that the skin on their feet eventually melds into these wire floors, making them unable to move. Their feet and legs become caked in feces.

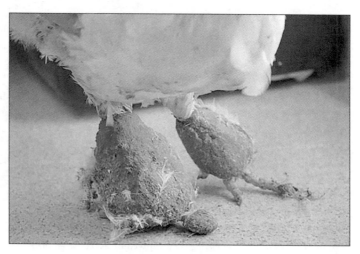

Feet Problems

This factory farm hen has lived in filth for so long that her feet are completely covered in dried feces. In situations like this, hens can get stuck to the bottom of their cages and, because they can't move, die from starvation or dehydration.

Cage Layer Osteoporosis

Broiler chickens (raised for their meat) have been genetically bred to get so big that many of these chickens have broken bones in their feet and legs because they are not strong enough to carry their weight. Interestingly, laying hens also have problems with their bones breaking, but for a much different reason.

It requires a lot of calcium to produce eggs, and as previously mentioned, laying hens are bred to make far more eggs than they would in a natural environment. In fact, factory farm hens are genetically and physically manipulated in many ways to lay eggs all year round instead of seasonally, which is normal for them. This excessively high level of egg production requires that calcium that would normally go to the hens' bones instead get used for egg production.

The combination of this high calcium demand for egg production and the fact that they get no exercise leads to a painful condition

Wire Floors

The wire floors of battery cages are very unnatural for chickens. Their feet can get stuck between the wires, or even "welded" to the wire floor if they are prevented from moving due to the crowded conditions. When these situations happen, hens cannot reach the food and water, and can die from starvation and dehydration.

known as cage layer osteoporosis. Like osteoporosis in humans, cage layer osteoporosis is a chronically painful disease that leads to brittle bones in hens. These brittle bones are highly susceptible to breaking,[48] and a hen can break a bone by simply hopping off a perch. One report found that keel bone fractures were nearly five times more common in battery cage hens than hens from other housing systems.[49] Another study of hens in battery cages found that 29% of the hens had newly broken bones just before they were slaughtered,[50] indicating rough treatment at the slaughterhouse in hens with very brittle bones.

ABNORMAL BEHAVIORS DUE TO CROWDING
Feather Pecking

Perhaps the worst problem in battery cage systems is feather pecking – not only for the condition itself, but because it is a precursor to cannibalism. As its name implies, feather pecking occurs when a hen repeatedly pecks at the feathers of another hen, pulling them out. Feather pecking is extremely common in battery cage systems.[51]

It is thought that feather pecking can occur as an act of aggression between hens, stemming from their frustration in not being able to establish a hierarchy (pecking order) amongst themselves in the extremely crowded conditions. It is also thought to happen as hens literally go crazy in these conditions, and start attacking other hens unprovoked. Perhaps most commonly, though, feather pecking occurs as re-directed behavior from their natural desire to peck the ground for food;[52] hens are so hard-wired to peck at the ground all day, that when there is no ground or substrate to peck, they will peck at each other.

Feather pecking is not only painful, but leads to skin wounds and bleeding; these wounds can incite the other birds to join in on the attack, and eventually lead to cannibalism. It can also result in open, pussy sores that can lead to infection. Feather pecking is considered a major problem in the egg industry, and interestingly, is an even bigger problem in cage-free systems, as we'll explore shortly.

Feather Pecking

Hens in nature are quite peaceful and live happily together. However, hens living in the tight quarters of a factory farm get psychologically distressed and can become very aggressive toward each other. Hens can have areas of their body completely devoid of feathers due to feather pecking from their aggressive cage mates. Extreme feather pecking can lead to cannibalism. About 7% - 15% of hens in factory farms are cannibalized by their fellow hens.

Photo Courtesy of Mercy for Animals

Cannibalism

Cannibalism is a completely abnormal behavior found most commonly in hens reared for egg production. It generally occurs after a hen has been a victim of extreme feather pecking. The feather pecking causes wounds which incite more feather pecking. Eventually, the pecking turns into cannibalization, when the pecking bird begins to eat the pecked bird. Several birds may join in. If the hen tries to escape, she draws attention to her plight, thus attracting more birds to join in.

Cannibalism is a major problem in battery cage systems, but is even worse in free-range and cage-free systems, as the hens have greater access to each other and are harder to control. Mortality rates due to cannibalism stand around 7% in battery cage systems, and can be as high as 15% in free -range systems.[53]

Vent Pecking

Similar to feather pecking, vent pecking occurs when a hen specifically pecks the cloaca (or "vent") of another hen. The cloaca is the area where the urogenital and intestinal tracts discharge.

Right after a hen lays an egg the cloaca is swollen and everted, exposing mucosa and bleeding from the tissue around the cloaca. Like any other open wound, a swollen and everted cloaca (vent) can incite other hens to peck it.

Vent pecking is very painful and causes tremendous stress to the hen being pecked. It can lead to skin tears, increasing the hen's likelihood of developing infection and disease, and can incite other hens to cannibalize her, leading to her death.

Prevalence rates show that 22% of hens in free-range systems, 10% in barn (cage-free) systems, and 6.2% in battery cages suffer from vent pecking.[54]

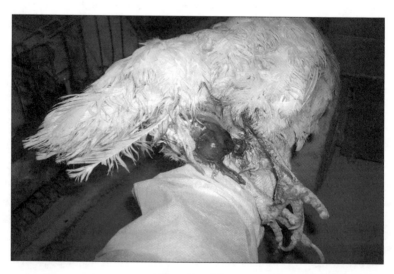

Vent Pecking

Vent pecking is the most common cause of cannibalism in egg-laying farms. Up to 22% of hens experience vent pecking on factory farms.

Photo Courtesy of Mercy for Animals

Autopsy research shows that the most common cause of death amongst laying hens is cannibalism (66%) with vent cannibalism the most common type (39%).[55]

Toe Pecking

Toe pecking is relatively rare, and occurs when one hen pecks the toes of another. It is thought to occur when a hen is physiologically stressed, and her adrenal glands in her feet become enlarged.[56] This incites other birds to peck her toes, and like other forms of pecking, can lead to cannibalism. Once again, toe pecking – like all forms of pecking – are rarely seen in natural environments.

Feather Plucking

Feather plucking is similar to feather pecking, except that the hen plucks out her own feathers. It is thought to occur when a bird's cage size restricts her movements, or when she is not allowed to exhibit her natural behaviors and becomes stressed.

Feather plucking has been likened to self-inflicted psychiatric disorders in humans, such as hair pulling. However, it could also be caused by conditions such as allergies or skin irritations, where the bird is trying to relieve her discomfort.

Sham or "Vacuum" Dustbathing

Sham dustbathing is another abnormal behavior seen in stressed hens in confinement. In sham dustbathing, the hen performs a typical dustbath as if she were outside on a farm, yet has no access to dust, litter, or any other substance with which to bathe.

Under normal conditions outside, adult hens will dustbathe approximately every other day, and each "bath" lasts about a half an hour. During the dustbath, the hen scratches the ground, erects her feathers and squats down. She then shakes her wings, rubs her head, rakes her bill and scratches with one leg. This process puts dirt into her feathers and then shakes it off. By doing this, the hen reduces the amount of feather lipids, which helps her feathers provide better insulation and also reduces skin parasites.[57]

However, in a battery cage system, hens live on a wire floor and do not have access to litter, dirt, or any other substance with which to bathe. Research shows that hens living on wire floors will often sham dustbathe near the food trough where they can peck and bill-rake the food,[58] apparently treating their food as a dustbathing substrate.

Stereotypy

A stereotypy is an abnormal behavior that involves repetitive movement. It is relatively common in people with mental disorders, as well as in animals caged into small areas such as zoos, research labs, and battery cages. A person who repetitively rocks, a lion who repetitively paces in his cage, and a hen who repetitively self-mutilates through feather plucking are all examples of stereotypies. In factory farms, hens can develop several types of stereotypies, including feather plucking and chewing on cage bars.

A stereotypy can be caused by many different things, such as a mental disorder, medication, or in the case of laying hens, highly unnatural living conditions where they cannot display their natural behaviors. Stereotypies are made worse by fatigue, stress and anxiety. It is not a natural condition found in hens living in a natural environment. Temple Grandin notes in her book *Animals Make Us Human* that these behaviors are very rare in nature, and when we see them in captive animals it almost always means that something is wrong.[59] Sadly, it is estimated that almost 83% of poultry worldwide suffer from stereotypies.[60]

Polydipsia

Polydipsia is another abnormal behavior seen in laying hens, although somewhat rare. Polydipsia is characterized by a hen drinking an excessive amount of water.

The cause of polydipsia in caged birds such as laying hens can be due to a variety of factors. One cause of polydipsia is zinc poisoning. The bars on many birdcages have a zinc coating, and hens can be exposed to zinc when living in the cages, especially if they have a stereotypy that involves repetitively chewing on cage bars. Another cause of polydipsia is a lesion in the supraoptic hypothalamus in the brain[61] that can occur if a hen is pecked by another bird in that area of her head. It can also occur due to stressful situations, such as crowded housing. In this latter case, it is called "psychogenic polydipsia."

Polydipsia is an abnormal behavior, and is not something that we would expect to see in hens living in natural conditions.

The Five Animal Freedoms

In the 1960's, the British Government commissioned a report on animal welfare in intensive animal production facilities, called the Brambell Report. This report outlined five basic freedoms that all animals should have in these production facilities:

1. Freedom from hunger and thirst
2. Freedom from discomfort
3. Freedom from pain, injury and disease
4. Freedom to express normal behavior
5. Freedom from fear and distress

It would be interesting to uncover what percentage of factory farms across the world actually provide these basic freedoms for their animals.

METHODS OF CONTROLLING ABNORMAL BEHAVIORS

It should be very apparent by now that the highly unnatural conditions of a factory farm cause an incredible amount of harm to the hens. These problems are extremely expensive for the factory owners, in terms of the high percentage of unusable "product" that results from these conditions.

In an attempt to lessen these expensive problems, factory farm owners employ a variety of different methods to help curtail injury and death, specifically due to feather pecking. These methods include beak trimming, light dimming, and installing perches.

Beak Trimming

To help minimize the issue of feather pecking and related injuries inflicted between birds, farm workers "trim" the birds' beaks by slicing off 1/3 – 2/3 of the beak with a sharp blade or an infra-red beam. While beak trimming does help reduce the rate of wounds and cannibalism amongst hens, it obviously isn't a great solution, given that an incredibly high number of hens still suffer from feather pecking and die from cannibalism, as we've discussed.[62]

There are many problems that arise from beak trimming. The most obvious problem with beak trimming is that it is extremely

Beak Trimming

Baby chicks have their beaks cut off, without anesthesia, when they are just a day or two old to help minimize feather plucking between chickens. This painful procedure can render hens unable to eat if their beaks are cut too short, and makes it harder for them to groom their feathers.

Photo courtesy of Mercy for Animals

cruel. No anesthetic is used when the beak is sliced off, and chicks' beaks have many sensitive nerve endings in them, so this procedure is extremely painful. Scientific evidence shows that beak trimming causes both acute and chronic pain. Noted Animal Behaviorist, Temple Grandin, attributes the reduced rate of feather pecking to pain avoidance – not lack of a beak.[63] Others add that beak trimming causes life-long chronic pain and discomfort and decreased ability to eat or drink.[64]

When a hen has had her beak trimmed, she has difficulty grooming herself. As we've learned, laying hens are packed together tightly in very dirty conditions. This creates a breeding ground for skin parasites: Hens with trimmed beaks have a bigger problem with skin parasites than hens with their beaks intact.[65]

Beak trimming can also lead to neuromas, which is abnormal nerve regeneration. Spontaneous neural discharges can occur from the beak, much like what happens when a human amputee has phantom limb pain.[66] Even though a large portion of the beak is missing, the hen still feels the pain.

Another very interesting fact about beak trimming is that chickens are capable of magnetoreception – the ability to orient themselves in relatively small areas based on the magnetic field of the earth.[67,68] However, their ability to do this lies in the iron mineral deposits in the dendrites in their upper beak. If this area of the beak is cut off, it raises the possibility that the hens will not be able to orient themselves in a cage-free system, or find their way in and out of a free-range building.[69]

One three year study showed that cannibalism rates in cage-free systems was 18% in birds with their beaks intact, but "only" 7% when the birds had their beaks trimmed.[70] This statistic may actually be much higher if you include vent cannibalization, which is often calculated separately.

Light Dimming

Another method that egg producers employ in their attempts to reduce feather pecking is simply dimming the lights so that the birds cannot see each other's wounds as easily. While this seems like an innocuous thing to do, it can actually cause quite a number of problems.

Hens will not lay eggs in the dark – they need to have a certain amount of light before they will produce eggs. When egg producers light the warehouses just enough to keep the hens laying eggs, but not enough for the hens to see each other's wounds, cloaca and other targets for pecking, it is not light enough for farm workers to inspect the birds. In fact, the lighting can be so low that workers cannot distinguish bloodstains from dirt stains on the hens. This could prevent hens from getting needed care.

If the workers turn on bright lights unexpectedly so they can conduct inspections, the hens become alarmed, and can start to panic. Feather pecking actually increases under these conditions[71] and widespread hysteria leads to further injuries.

Poultry bred in factory farming conditions where light dimming has been employed have been shown to suffer from detached retinas and buphthalmia, a distortion of the eye morphology.[72,73] Both conditions can lead to blindness.

Finally, hens have been shown to prefer to eat in brightly lit environments,[74] and also prefer lightness for times when they are active, and darkness when they are inactive.[75]

Despite all of these problems, light dimming is commonly used among egg producers.

Perches

In nature, chickens like to perch and sleep in trees, but of course, there are no trees inside factory farms. However, it is possible to put perches into battery cages if the cages are large enough. When baby chicks are reared with perches in their cages, they are more likely to use them, and increased rates of perching are associated with decreased rates of cannibalism,[76] especially vent cannibalism, as it is harder for a hen to reach another hen's cloaca if she is on a perch. Subordinate hens also fare better with perches, as they don't get feather pecked as much.[77] However, perches take up valuable square footage, which leads to lower revenues, so very few egg farmers provide perches at this time.

EFFICIENCIES ON A FACTORY FARM
Hatcheries

As hens die or are slaughtered on a factory farm, new hens need to replace them, so hatcheries exist to breed layer hens.

A shocking fact that stems specifically from egg production is that these hatcheries have no use for male chicks; not only can the males not lay eggs, but since laying hens are not bred to grow big and meaty like broiler chickens, they don't make for good chicken meat either. Therefore, all the male chicks born into hatcheries are killed just after birth.

There are two main methods that these baby chicks are killed: One method is to toss the chicks into a grinder where they will be ground up alive; the second method is to toss them into a dumpster or garbage bag where they will slowly suffocate as other chicks are tossed on top of them.

Male chicks falling from the conveyor belt into the grinder
Laying hens are bred to lay eggs, and are quite small. Therefore, they do not make for good meat. Baby male chicks are therefore not useful to the industry – they will never be able to lay eggs and are not worth the money to raise them for the paltry amount of meat they will provide. Therefore, shortly after they are born, they are ground up alive or thrown in a dumpster to suffocate.
Photo Courtesy of Mercy for Animals

Eating eggs – even cage free and free range eggs – directly creates demand for laying hens and hatcheries, which results in millions of baby male chicks being killed each year.

Forced Molting

After a hen has gone through a full season laying eggs, her production rates can begin to drop in the second and third laying season. One way to increase a hen's production rate is through a process called "forced molting" or "induced molting."

Molting is a term that describes periodic feather shedding that occurs at certain times of the year or at certain times in the life cycle of an animal. For example, when snakes shed their skin once or twice a year, they are molting.

Similarly, chickens molt their feathers as old feathers become worn down and need to be replaced. In nature, chickens generally molt old feathers in the autumn, although they can molt more than once in a given year. They do not molt all of their feathers at once because they need feathers for insulation and to repel water, so in nature, molting is a relatively slow process. Chickens will molt a handful of feathers at a time, and as those feathers grow in they will molt some more, always ensuring that they have enough feathers for insulation and water repellent during the molt. Bald spots do not naturally occur from molting.

In nature, hens generally molt right after the breeding season. Because feathers make up 4-12% of a bird's weight, it takes a large amount of energy to molt, so hens will not lay eggs until they are finished molting and their feathers have grown back in. This also allows a hen's reproductive tract to recover and rejuvenate.

In egg production facilities, however, egg producers have found that by forcing a hen to molt they can re-invigorate her egg production levels. Because egg producers do not want to keep a hen out of "production" for long, they force her to molt all of her feathers at once.

To force a molt, hens are starved of most or all of their food and water for up to 14 days. A hen's weight will drop by 30-35%. This

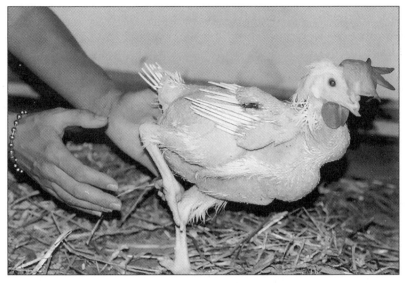

Forced Molt

To increase egg production and make more profit for the farmers,
hens are forced to molt all their feathers at once – an extremely
cruel and unnatural condition for chickens.

Photo Courtesy of Mercy for Animals

will deplete specific nutrients and shock her body, and she will quit laying eggs and lose all of her feathers[78] – a "forced molt." Some hens will die due to this forced molting process.[79]

During the molt, her reproductive tract will have time to rejuvenate, so that when she is ready to start making eggs again, she will make them near her peak levels and her egg quality will be improved.

Forcing hens to molt is a way for egg producers to squeeze as many eggs out of a hen in her latter seasons as they can before sending her to slaughter. Forced molting through withholding feed and water is outlawed in the United Kingdom and essentially obsolete in Canada, but perfectly accepted in the United States. In early 2003, over 75% of the egg laying hens in the U.S. were forced to molt.[80]

CAGE-FREE, FREE-RANGE AND ORGANIC EGGS

Many people who care about animals wonder, "What's wrong with eating cage-free, free-range or organic eggs? Aren't the animals treated well in these conditions?" It's a good question. Many of us believe that if you want to avoid hormones and chemicals in your eggs, you should buy organic, and if you want to avoid animal cruelty, you should buy cage-free or free-range eggs. That's exactly what the egg producers are hoping you will believe. However, here's what you need to know...

Cage-Free and Free-Range Eggs

The terms "cage-free" and "free range" evoke a good feeling in most people. It evokes an image of chickens that are "free" out on a "range." Yet in many cases, nothing could be further from the truth.

In most countries, the term "cage-free" only means that the birds do not live in a cage. However, they are still extremely crowded, living in a huge warehouse covered in feces and filth, and not allowed access to the outdoors.

Cage Free

The term "cage free" conjurs up images of hens on a farm, pecking the ground and nesting in trees. However, in the vast majority of cases, the hens are stuffed together just as tightly as in battery cages – they just don't have wire bars around them – and they are not allowed access to the outdoors.

"Free-range" often only means that the birds are not in cages and are permitted to roam free within a farmyard, a shed or a chicken coop that has some access to the outdoors. In many cases, though, a free-range "farm" is just a large warehouse that has a tiny door at the far end with a small area outside where the chickens are permitted to go. However, if a hen is not living anywhere near the door, she will likely never even know it is there! Even if she lives closer to the end with a door, it is so crowded that she may still never know the door is there or if she does, she may not be able to reach it.

In the U.S., the USDA only requires that the free-range birds spend "a part of their time outside." The five-minute trip when a hen gets moved from the hatchery to the warehouse meets this USDA standard.

Furthermore, what many people don't know – and the egg producers certainly don't want you to find out – is that hens in a free-range or cage-free system have the same problems – and sometimes worse – than caged hens. Just like caged hens, they do not have room to move about sufficiently, and do not have the ability to establish a hierarchy (called a "pecking order.") Just like hens in battery cages, they experience severe crowding that leads to many abnormal behaviors and psychological stresses.

In fact, feather pecking and cannibalism are more common in cage free and free-range systems than in battery cage systems. This is because it is harder to control the hens, and the behavior can spread more quickly amongst the birds. Prevalence figures of feather pecking in free-range flocks range between 57% to 86%.[81,82,83] Due to this increased rate of feather pecking, hens in these cageless systems actually have a higher rate of cannibalism than those in battery cages.[84]

On the next page notice all the same challenges that hens face in caged, cage-free and free-range systems. (Table 2.1)

An important distinction to remember is that cage-free does not mean cruelty-free. Most cage-free hens still have their beaks cut off, are still pumped full of antibiotics and hormones, still suffer from infection, feather pecking, vent pecking, cannibalism, stereotypies and other injuries and disorders.

Table 2.1: Conditons Affecting Commercially Raised Hens

HARMFUL CONDITIONS AFFECTING BATTERY CAGE, CAGE-FREE AND FREE-RANGE HENS		
	Battery Cage	Cage-Free	Free-Range
Crowding	✔	✔	✔
Infections	✔	✔	✔
Feet Problems	✔	✔	✔
Cage Layer Osteoporosis	✔	✔	✔
Feather Pecking	✔	✔	✔
Cannibalism	✔	✔	✔
Vent Pecking	✔	✔	✔
Feather Plucking	✔	✔	✔
Toe Pecking	✔	✔	✔
Stereotypies	✔	✔	✔
Polydipsia	✔	✔	✔
Sham Dustbathing	✔	✔	✔
Beak Trimming	✔	✔	✔
Forced Molting	✔	✔	✔
Male Chicks Killed	✔	✔	✔

Furthermore, "free-range" and "cage-free" do not imply that the hens were fed any differently than on normal commercial farms. Like their brothers and sisters in battery cages, cage-free and free-range hens can be fed the same animal derived byproducts and genetically modified foods. Only eggs marked "organic" can be assured to come from hens that were fed an organic diet.

In an ideal free-range setting, hens would have plenty of access to the outdoors without experiencing crowding from too many hens on the farm. They would be able to forage for their natural diet,

Free Range

*The term "free range" conjurs up images of hens on a farm,
pecking the ground and nesting in trees. However, in the vast majority
of cases, the hens are stuffed together just as tightly as in battery cages –
they just don't have wire bars around them – and while they are
allowed access to the outdoors, they may never actually see the
outdoors more than once or twice in their lives.*

live in clean conditions, sleep in trees and exhibit all of their natural behaviors such as dust bathing and foraging. Although many of us assume this happens with free-range hens, it is rarely the case.

The U.S. government does not have standards in place to ensure the eggs labeled "free-range" actually come from hens in a natural environment. Many free-range farms still are extremely crowded, and as noted above, feather pecking and its related atrocities – like cannibalism – are actually higher in free-range systems than in battery cage systems. Beak trimming is still standard business on free-range farms, and diseases and infection are common.

Finally, don't forget that most free-range hens come from the same hatcheries that kill all the baby male chicks in a grinder or through suffocation. Therefore, by trying to do the right thing and supporting the "cage-free" and "free-range" egg producers, consumers are inadvertently supporting the death of millions of baby male chicks every year.

Organic Eggs

When speaking of organic eggs, the word "organic" only implies standards set with regard to feed and medicine. Hens raised in an organic system must be fed organic feed, and also must not be given antibiotics or other drugs.

While this sounds positive and natural, it rarely is. There is nothing that says hens in an organic system must also get to roam free in a large area, feel sunlight on their backs or get to dust bathe or perch in trees. The truth is that organic eggs, in most places, still come from hens in the same horrible, crowded conditions as cage-free and free-range hens.

Furthermore, as we've discussed, these filthy conditions breed disease. The hens often need antibiotics and other medications to treat these diseases but as soon as a hen receives antibiotics or medications, her eggs can no longer be called "organic," so the farmers have an incentive not to give them medication. Therefore, many hens suffer with infections and illnesses that could be treated in a non-organic situation.

When you see stickers claiming "Cage-Free" or "Free-Range" or "Organic" – don't be fooled:

"Cage-Free,"
"Free-Range"
and "Organic"
do not imply Cruelty Free.

Finally, do not be fooled by "cruelty free" claims either – there are absolutely no laws or standards around using this label, and no one is enforcing it. Furthermore, even if a farm is careful to be humane, they are still responsible for creating demand that kills many baby male chicks if they get their chicks from a hatchery.

SLAUGHTER

After living a terrible life, most likely never feeling the sun or the rain on her feathers, never pecking the dirt, never spreading her wings, and constantly being pecked and attacked by fellow birds, a hen still gets slaughtered in the exact same place that broiler chickens are slaughtered.

Sadly, chickens are excluded from the Humane Methods of Slaughter Act.[85] In most cases, a hen's slaughter begins when she is placed on a moving conveyer belt in the air, held upside down by her fragile legs, which often break under her weight. She will be dragged upside down along a conveyer line until she is over the electrified water bath, where her head will be lowered into the water and she will be electrocuted. This is supposed to kill her or render her unconscious before she is slaughtered. However, many hens are still alive and fully conscious when they are lifted out of the electric bath, and like dairy cows, are slaughtered alive.

CONCLUSION

A lot of vegetarians eat eggs, not knowing what billions of hens go through to provide eggs for their omelets and the baked goods they love to eat. Perhaps even worse, many well-meaning people spend their hard-earned money because they've been fooled by the egg industry into believing that cage-free, free-range and organic labels mean that the hens have been treated well. As you've just learned, that is nearly always a fallacy.

Almost all hens in factory farms – whether they live in cages or are "free range" – suffer from a myriad of issues that are almost exclusive to the crowded and unsanitary conditions of factory farms: Infections, feet problems, cage layer osteoporosis, feather pecking, vent pecking, cannibalism, toe pecking, feather plucking, stereotypies, polydipsia, and sham dustbathing. And, of course, there are the harmful results of standard factory farm practices like beak trimming, light dimming and forced molting. Finally, in what many people consider the most inhumane activity in all the food industry, tiny male chicks are tossed alive into grinders and dumpsters, their sex deeming them useless to the farmers.

Now that you know the facts, make it a point to read ingredient labels and notice how often eggs show up food products. When you begin to realize just how many eggs you are consuming in the course of a given year, you will understand just how many hens you can save from suffering in factory farms … and how many countless male baby chicks you can save from being killed alive. You can change everything going forward, by vowing to eliminate eggs as you finish this chapter.

"Never, never be afraid to do what's right,
especially if the well-being of a person or
animal is at stake. Society's punishments are
small compared to the wounds we inflict on
our soul when we look the other way."
– Martin Luther King

Chapter 3

HONEY

Honey has caused a big debate amongst vegans: Is it vegan, or is it not? The answer simply depends on how you define vegan. Those who define a vegan diet as devoid of animal products may claim that a honeybee is an insect, not an animal, and therefore honey is indeed a vegan product. However, those who believe that a vegan diet is devoid of products that exploit any sentient being would argue that an insect is simply another form of life, and should be respected just as much as an animal, fish or fowl; thus, honey is not vegan. Therefore, to decide whether honey is vegan, you need to decide how you define "vegan." However, let's shed some light on honeybees, to help you make a decision about whether you want to eat honey.

It's been said that bees are more important to our planet than humans. Bees are essential to thousands species on Earth – including humans – because they pollinate the flowers of fruit trees. Without pollinated flowers, there is no fruit on most fruit trees. So, without bees, we have little or no fruit. About a third of all U.S. crops depend on bees to pollinate them, and many plants on the endangered species list are endangered specifically because they are not getting pollinated.

Why are these plants not getting pollinated? Because the bee population has been dying off quickly and dramatically. Domestically managed bee colonies have dropped by half since 1945,[86] and much of this has happened in the past decade. While the cause of these deaths was a mystery for many years (some theorized it was due to cell phone emissions, viruses, and other causes) it is now widely believed in the beekeeping industry that this massive collapse of bee colonies is due to the use of systemic pesticides. Systemic pesticides are not sprayed on crops like traditional pesticides – they are "built in" to the seeds so that when the plants grows, they have the pesticide inside of them, and farmers don't have to spray.

Interestingly, beekeepers do not make most of their money from honey. Because bee populations are now so rare, and because huge, industrial-sized agricultural farms have thousands of acres of crops that desperately need to be pollinated, beekeepers literally truck their bees around the country and "rent" their bees out for a few months at a time to farmers. This is where they make the majority of their money. A beekeeper living in Florida might truck his hives to California to pollinate an avocado farm, then a few months later drive to Washington to pollinate an apple orchard, and then a few months later drive to Maine to pollinate a cranberry farm.

This practice of moving bees from state to state and climate to climate is not natural for them. It also involves a lot of energy to raise bees and truck them all over the country, which isn't very good for our environment. Additionally, the bees' honey, which in nature is made by bees for bees, is taken from them to be sold to humans, and they are given a form of sugar-water to eat instead. While this may or may not be bad for them, one can only imagine that their own honey is the absolute best thing for their health ... just like mother's milk is better for a baby than formula.

From a health standpoint, many people argue that because honey is mainly made up of fructose (38.5%) and glucose (31%), which is a similar ratio to inverted sugar syrup, it is essentially just another simple sugar, so we should avoid it. On the other hand, honey is known to have very small amounts of compounds that are thought to act as antioxidants.[87,88] Honey is also thought to have an anti-allergenic effect, and be helpful in a variety of medical areas like scar healing. Steve Blake, Author and Doctor of Holistic Health in Nutritional Biochemistry, confirms that honey is actually healthy in small quantities – although he doesn't eat it. He says, "Honey is unusual in that it is a healthful non-vegan food. Raw, unfiltered honey contains propolis, which is a powerful antimicrobial. The pollen in unfiltered honey is also very nutritious and energizing." However, Steve does not eat honey as a vegan because, he says, "flower pollen is available directly, without bothering any bees."

The ethics of insects is not necessarily straightforward. Some ethicists argue that people probably kill a good number of insects on their windshields while driving to the store to buy honey! Others point out that if a vegan staunchly says we should not kill insects then they should also never eat conventional (non-organic) produce, which is covered in pesticides, whose main purpose is, of course … to kill insects.

However, even if you don't get the warm-fuzzies for insects, ask yourself if you should respect their lives any less? Given that they essentially feed billions of humans and animals abundantly with most of the fruit on Earth, it's hard to argue that they are inconsequential beings. Even if you kill insects on your car windshield or indirectly through eating conventional produce, you can still make a conscious decision to do your absolute best (even though it may not be perfect) to avoid doing things that put other creatures – even insects – in harm's way. There are many alternatives to honey that can be used to sweeten foods, like agave nectar, molasses, and many others. Eating honey is simply not necessary.

"People eat meat and think
they will become as strong as an ox,
forgetting that the ox eats grass."
– Pino Caruso

Chapter 4
DAIRY, EGGS AND YOUR HEALTH

We have been taught from a young age that dairy and egg products – especially low-fat dairy products – are healthy for us. Dairy has become synonymous with calcium, and almost everyone will tell you that dairy products are good for our bones. The government actually *requires* that milk is offered in our school lunch programs to our children. We are also taught that eggs are the "perfect protein," and that it is healthy to eat eggs several times a week. But like our ancestors who believed the Earth was flat, is it possible that we are wrong?

Some doctors and researchers are starting to argue that we have been absolutely brainwashed to believe that "milk does a body good," that eggs are the perfect protein, and that we need dairy products so we have calcium for strong bones. They are pointing to a growing body of scientific evidence that suggests dairy products are associated with all kinds of diseases and maladies. Could they be right? The best way to decide is to look at that body of scientific evidence for ourselves … and, indeed, there is an incredible amount of evidence that dairy and egg products are not healthy after all.

DAIRY AND CANCER
Dairy and Cancer: Animal Protein
Cancer has become ubiquitous in our modern society. Despite billions of dollars poured into research, we still don't know much about what causes it, and we still don't know how to cure it.

A groundbreaking book called *The China Study*,[89] by T. Colin Campbell, PhD, is one of the best sources of scientific evidence that outlines the link between cancer and dairy products. Dr. Campbell began his career many decades ago with an aim to find the highest quality protein to help feed starving people most efficiently, and assumed this "highest quality" protein would naturally come from animal meat. But as he read the medical literature, he came across one particular study that would change the entire course of his career. This study, in fact, did not back up his theory that animal protein was the highest quality protein for consumption – it concluded exactly the opposite: that animal protein caused cancer.

In this study, 60 rats were given a cancer-causing substance called aflatoxin, and were then divided into two groups:

- Group 1 received a "regular diet" that included 20% of total calories from animal-based protein (they used a type of protein called casein, most commonly found in dairy products).

- Group 2 received a "low protein" diet, which included only 5% of calories from protein (also from casein.)

The hypothesis of the study was that those who had more animal protein in their diet would be healthier, and thus better able to ward off cancer or pre-cancerous cell clusters (called "foci") after being exposed to the cancer-causing substance, aflatoxin.

Incredibly, they found the exact opposite: Literally *all* of the rats fed the 20% high-protein diet developed cancer or pre-cancerous cells, while *none* of the rats on the 5% low-protein diet developed cancer or pre-cancerous cells.[90] (Table 4.1)

Table 4.1: Dietary Protein and AFB1 Induced Liver Cancer (Rats)

Dietary Protein %	Animals with Tumors and Hyperplastic Nodules
20%	30/30 (100%)
5%	0/30 (0%)

Source: Madhavan TV, and Gopalan C. 1968

This type of "all or nothing" result is very rare in scientific studies. In fact, it is so rare that most scientists would conclude that something was wrong with the study methods or the study design! So Dr. Campbell and his colleagues decided to recreate the study in over 100 rats. Not only did they find the same results, but they also expanded the study to show that if you let the tumors grow for 100 weeks, all the animals fed the 20% protein diet were dead or nearly dead from liver tumors, but all of the rats fed the 5% low-protein diet were still alive![91] (Table 4.2)

Table 4.2: Dietary Protein and
Aflatoxin-Induced Liver Cancer at 100 Weeks

Dietary Protein %	Alive at 100 Weeks
20%	0/58 (0%)
5%	60/60 (100%)

Source: Madhavan TV, and Gopalan C. 1968

Perhaps the most intriguing part of his studies, however, was when Dr. Campbell and colleagues' studied the effects of switching the protein content back and forth: In this study, they took rats and fed them a 20% animal protein diet, and then switched them back to a 5% animal protein diet, then switched them back to a 20% animal protein diet and then finally switched them back to a 5% animal protein diet. What they found was that they could essentially turn cancer on and off like a light switch by varying the protein amounts in the diet every 3 weeks: Every time the rats were fed the high-protein diet they began to develop pre-cancerous lesions, but when they were switched back to a low-protein diet the lesions all or mostly went away! They could basically turn cancer on and off by varying the amount of animal protein in the rats' diet!

While these results were astounding to Dr. Campbell, there was still a big unanswered question: Was it protein in general that was causing this cancerous effect, or was it specifically animal-based protein that was causing this effect? To test this question, Dr. Campbell and his colleagues re-created the studies, but instead of using the animal protein casein, they used soy protein and wheat protein – both of which are plant-based. As it turned out, neither soy nor wheat protein caused any cancer or pre-cancerous cells – even at levels of 20% of total calories!

These data are extremely compelling, and offer a tremendous amount of hope to those of us who may get a diagnosis of cancer; perhaps if we catch it quickly and then radically lower or eliminate our animal protein intake, we can turn the cancer "off" and watch it disappear. Certainly, there are many examples of people who have done exactly this.

Ruth Heidrich

Ruth Heidrich has a PhD in Health Management, so she understands good health. She had always been athletic, ate what most people would consider a very healthy diet, and described herself as the fittest person she knew.

Nevertheless, at 47 Dr. Heidrich was diagnosed with breast cancer. The cancer had already spread to her bones and lung, making it an instant Stage IV diagnosis. When doctors suggested chemotherapy and other traditional treatments, she decided instead to follow a very low-fat vegan diet.

Without any traditional medical treatments, Dr. Heidrich completely overcame the cancer, and has been cancer-free for over 20 years. She now runs an average of 70 races per year, has over 900 Gold medals from various races, is a six-time Ironman Triathlon finisher, holds three world records in fitness, and is an eight-time Senior Olympic Gold medalist. In 1999 she was named one of the "Top Ten Fittest Women in North America."

Interestingly, after all of these studies, Dr. Campbell found himself in a quandary. Remember that his original goal was to try to find a way to feed the world's poorest people, and he had set out to prove that feeding them the "highest quality" protein (from animal sources) was the best way to do this. But he'd found just the opposite: it seemed that animal protein was causing cancer ... at least in rats. But rats aren't humans, and studies done in animals often do not yield the same results in humans. Dr. Campbell needed data from humans to see if the results in his rat studies would carry over to humans.

So Dr. Campbell starting looking at humans. As he looked across the Philippines where he had focused his attention for his work, he found a similar pattern in humans as he had in the rats: those who came from wealthier families and could afford to eat a relatively high amount of animal protein tended to be the ones who developed liver cancer; those who came from the poor areas and could not afford to eat meat or other animal proteins did not get liver cancer.

Dr. Campbell and his colleagues went on to lead the world's largest epidemiological study in nutrition, The China Study, which the New York Times called the "grand prix" of epidemiological nutrition research. Essentially, what they found was that in 6,500 Chinese people from 65 counties across China, those who lived in the rural areas and ate a diet of mainly rice and vegetables (very low in animal protein) rarely got cancer; but those who lived in wealthier areas and ate more animal protein in their diets got cancer most often.

Since the researchers couldn't control for every factor, many wonder if it could have been something other than the animal protein that caused this: Perhaps genetics played a role? Perhaps the people living in rural areas got more exercise working in the fields, and the increased exercise helped to ward off cancer? As it turned out, genetics were similar across the country, and exercise (as well as many other factors) could be explained away statistically. When the researchers looked at every factor they could think of and statistically controlled for all of those elements, nothing else was shown to be a significant factor in people's rates of cancer except the animal protein they ate.

Dairy and Cancer: Animal Fat

Like with animal protein, we see a similar story when we look at research involving animal fat and cancer rates. Most of us have heard that fatty diets are highly linked to heart disease and many cancers. But let's ask another question: Is it really a fatty diet that is linked to cancer, or is it an *animal* fatty diet that is linked to cancer?

In a large-scale observational study, Carroll and his colleagues researched the correlation between animal fat, plant fat and cancer, and found that animal fat was highly linked to breast cancer, but plant fat was not.[92] (Figure 4.1)

However, before concluding that animal fat causes cancer, you must notice that where you find animal fat, you are probably going to find high levels of animal protein as well. Thus, a new question arises: Is it animal fat, or could it be animal protein (or both), that increases people's risk of cancer?

To help find this answer, let's look at the famous Nurse's Health Study.[93] This study got a lot of attention because it was such a large and well-controlled study. Over 88,000 nurses were followed for over more than 20 years to look for links between disease and dietary patterns. When the results were announced, this study got even more attention – they found no link between fat intake and breast cancer! This was completely contradictory to all the other evidence in the medical literature. Study after study had linked high fat intake to increased breast cancer rates, so how could this large-scale, well-designed study possibly show that women who ate more than 49% of their calories from fat had no difference in breast cancer rates than those who ate less than 29% of their calories from fat?

Here is one answer: The study noted that as people's fat intake decreased, their protein intake increased. For example, when a person replaces high-fat milk with non-fat milk in their diet, the non-fat milk has a higher percentage of protein (casein) in it, so they were inadvertently increasing their protein intake when they decreased their fat. As we have just seen in the preceding pages, casein is highly linked to cancer. So, both those with a high fat diet and a low-fat (high protein) diet had similar rates of cancer.

Figure 4.1: Animal Fat Intake,
Plant Fat Intake and Breast Cancer Risk.

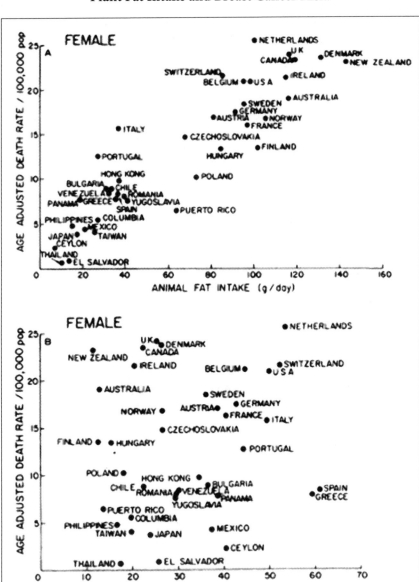

Source: Carroll KK. *Experimental Evidence of dietary factors and hormone-dependent cancers.* Cancer Res 1975;35:3374-3383.

Another very likely answer as to why there was no difference in cancer rates between the high-fat diet group and the low-fat diet group could be that 29% of calories from fat is not "low-fat" at all! It is quite possible that 29% of calories from fat is high enough to cause cancer at the same rate that a "high-fat" diet causes cancer.

Let's look at even more evidence. Like Dr. Carroll, Ganmaa and colleagues found the same high correlation between drinking cow's milk and both breast and uterine cancer.[94] (Figure 4.2) This could be due to fat or animal protein intake, and/or increased levels of hormones, as you'll read in the next section.

Figure 4.2: Cow's Milk Intake and Breast Cancer and Uterine Cancer Risk

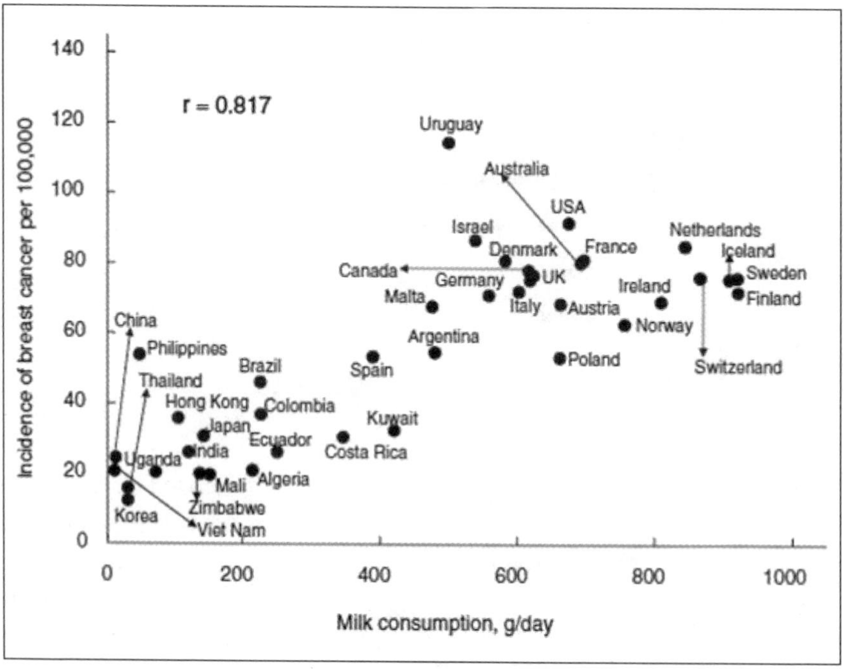

Source: Ganmaa D and Sato A, *The possible role of female sex hormones in milk from pregnant cows in the development of breast, ovarian and corpus uteri cancers.* Med Hypotheses. 2005;65(6):1028-37.

You won't find casein or any other animal protein in plant foods, but you'll find it in high levels in dairy products. If you are eating a vegetarian diet, chances are that you have swapped out meat and fish for cheese and other dairy products. Instead of ordering spaghetti and meatballs, you may order fettuccine alfredo; instead of having a turkey sandwich, you might have a grilled cheese sandwich. Filled with high levels of animal protein and fat, dairy products put vegetarians at risk of getting cancer.

The protein in cow's milk is designed for baby cows, just like the protein in human milk is designed for baby humans. A baby calf grows from 60 pounds to 600 pounds in just one year – that's a 10 fold increase in size. But baby humans only grow from about 7 pounds to 20 pounds in their first year – about a 3-fold increase in size. The amount of protein in cow's milk is designed to make baby cows grow very big, very fast. That may be fine if you're a baby cow, but not if you're a human. What appears to happen instead is cow's milk helps not only healthy human cells multiply quickly, but it helps cancer cells multiply quickly as well.

Dairy and Cancer: Hormones

A topic that has been getting attention lately is the link between hormone-related cancers and foods that contain naturally occurring hormones in them. Certain cancers are associated with organs that have high levels of hormones, such as breast cancer, ovarian cancer and uterine cancer.

Cow's milk has very high levels of hormones in it, and researchers are now getting concerned that these high levels of hormones are increasing the incidence of hormone-related cancers. If humans have been drinking cow's milk for thousands of years, why would cancer rates be increasing now? The answer lies in factory farming methods. Unlike cows in pastures before the advent of factory farms, cows today are kept pregnant and forced to lactate throughout their pregnancy. Milk that comes from a cow in the latter half of her pregnancy has higher concentrations of estrogen and progesterone in it.

Researchers in Japan hypothesized that these higher levels of estrogen and progesterone are responsible for the increasing incidence and death from hormone-related cancers. Indeed, when they looked at 40 countries and correlated their food intake with cancer rates, they found that:[95]

- There was a correlation of 82.7% between breast cancer and meat
- There was a correlation of 817% between breast cancer and milk
- There was a correlation of 75.1% between breast cancer and cheese
- There was a correlation of 77.9% between ovarian cancer and milk
- There was a correlation of 71.7% between ovarian cancer and animal fat
- There was a correlation of 69.7% between ovarian cancer and cheese
- There was a correlation of 81.4% between uterine cancer and milk
- There was a correlation of 78.7% between uterine cancer and cheese

With these astonishing results, the researchers concluded, "increased consumption of animal-derived food may have adverse effects on the development of hormone-dependent cancers. Among dietary risk factors, we are most concerned with milk and dairy products, because the milk we drink today is produced from pregnant cows, in which estrogen and progesterone levels are markedly elevated."[96]

Dairy and Cancer: Insulin-Like Growth Factor-1

In our understanding of dairy's link to cancer, let's finish by discussing Insulin-Like Growth Factor-1 (IGF-1). Don't be intimidated by the scientific-sounding name; if you focus on the words "Growth

Factor" you'll remember that IGF-1 is simply a hormone found in your body that helps things grow.

IGF-1 has growth-promoting effects on almost every cell in the body, and also regulates cell growth and development. Therefore, IGF-1 is important for fetal and childhood growth, but in adults, it promotes the aging process. Since fetuses and children grow rapidly, a mother's milk is full of IGF-1. This is true of human milk as well as cow's milk. However, when we become an adult, our body doesn't need to grow as much anymore, and we don't need to consume such levels of IGF-1.

Not only do adults not need to consume high levels of IGF-1, it has actually been found to be harmful. You may be aware that our bodies make cancerous cells every day, but a healthy body's immune system finds these cancerous cells and kills them off quickly so they never replicate and become problematic. However, if given the right environment – such as a sickly body with high levels of growth-promoting IGF-1 in it – one little cancer cell can win the fight against the immune system, and will divide multiple times until it eventually turns into full-blown cancer. Since IGF-1 is a growth factor, high levels of IGF-1 in adults help cancerous cells to grow and grow. Perhaps not surprisingly, high levels of IGF-1 are also linked to high levels of vascular endothelial growth factor (VEGF) – another growth factor – that actually helps to grow new blood vessels to feed the tumors with blood and oxygen!

According to Joseph Keon, PhD, "IGF-1 is one of the hottest topics in cancer research today." No wonder – it turns out that IGF-1 is *required* for tumor formation, and it's *required* for metastases to occur (the process when a tumor that began in one place spreads to other organs in the body.)

So, like animal protein, IGF-1 not only helps "good" cells to grow, like bone and muscle cells, but it also helps the "bad" cells to grow ... like cancer cells. It's now thought that IGF-1 is a strong predictor of cancer, just like cholesterol is a strong predictor of heart disease.

To link hypothesis to reality, let's turn from research on IGF-1 in the lab to research on humans. A diet high in dairy products is associated with higher levels of circulating IGF-1 in the body. Several studies have shown that increased levels of IGF-1 lead to an increased growth of cancer cells,[97] and that the amount of IGF-1 in the liver is positively associated with a diet high in casein, while low IGF-1 levels were associated with a casein-free diet.[98]

Here is some proof from human studies that dairy products are likely putting people at an increased risk for cancer:

- Pre-menopausal women with the highest circulating levels of IGF-1 have a 7-fold greater risk of breast cancer when compared with women who have the lowest rates of IGF-1.[99]

- Men under 60 with the highest circulating levels of IGF-1 have a 4-fold greater risk of prostate cancer when compared with men who have the lowest rates of IGF-1.[100]

- Women with high IGF-1 levels had a higher rate of getting colorectal cancer.[101]

- Women who consumed more than one glass of milk per day had a 73 percent greater chance of ovarian cancer than women who drank less than one glass per day.[102]

- Men who drank two or more glasses of milk a day were almost twice as likely to develop advanced prostate cancer as those who didn't drink milk at all.[103]

- Men who had 2 ½ servings of dairy products a day had a 34% increased risk of prostate cancer, compared to those who had little or not dairy consumption.[104]

Again, if you are eating a vegetarian diet that includes dairy products (which all start as milk,) you are likely putting yourself at risk for cancer, not only by eating animal protein, but by also increasing the amount of IGF-1 in your body.

If you love your life and want to live it healthfully, ask yourself just how much you love your dairy products. If you have kids and believe milk is healthy for children, note this statistic: Three servings of milk a day will raise IGF-1 levels by 10%.[105]

DAIRY, EGGS AND HEART DISEASE

Let's turn our attention from cancer to another leading cause of death – heart disease. Dairy and egg products contain a lot of cholesterol and fat, both of which are highly linked to heart disease. In fact, egg yolks have one of the highest levels of cholesterol of any food on the planet and cheese has 70-80% of its calories from fat, most of which is from saturated (bad) fat. Fatty and cholesterol-laden diets have been cited repeatedly in medical literature to cause heart disease.[106]

Heart disease – particularly heart attacks – is mostly a disease of blood vessels more so than the heart. When high levels of fat and cholesterol continually enter the blood stream, the arteries can build up plaque that, over time, can completely clog up the affected artery, much like a sink drain can get clogged. While clogging an entire artery with a large plaque can take years or decades to happen, it turns out that little plaques on the side of an artery can break off from the artery wall and form a blood clot, which can then clog the artery just like a large plaque would.

When an artery gets completely blocked, blood – and the precious oxygen it carries – cannot flow to the heart. It is this lack of oxygen to the heart that causes a heart attack. Therefore, when we talk about heart attacks, it's really the vessels that are diseased, which leads to a clot that blocks blood and oxygen from getting to the heart. Similarly, when an artery leading to the brain gets blocked, it causes an ischemic stroke.

Saturated fat is particularly dangerous in clogging up the arteries, and more than 27% of America's saturated fat intake currently comes from dairy products and eggs.[107] But the jury still seems to be out over just how much fat is safe for your heart. The USDA 2010 guidelines allow for 20-35% of an adult's diet to come from fat, including a full 10% from saturated fat.[108]

Curiously, the Women's Health Initiative Study,[109] which studied women on a "low-fat" diet of 29% fat, found that there was no benefit of a "low-fat" diet on rates of heart attacks, strokes, breast cancer and colon cancer when compared to those who ate whatever they wanted. However, as mentioned earlier, many doctors are now pointing out that this doesn't tell us that a low-fat diet doesn't work; it tells us that a diet of 29% fat is not a low-fat diet.

In another famous study that made the "Mediterranean Diet" so popular, The Lyon Diet Heart Study[110] studied 605 patients that had already survived one heart attack. The patients in the treatment group were told to eat a "Mediterranean Diet," high in fish, fruits, vegetables, breads, beans, nuts, and seeds. They were told to go light on dairy products, poultry, meat, eggs, and wine. They were also told to add in olive oil, for its monounsaturated fats. About 30% of this diet was from fat. The patients in the control group were given no dietary advice, and ate a diet typical of most Westerners, particularly high in saturated fat. Their total fat intake was about 34% – the same as most Americans.

The study had seemingly very good results: The people on the Mediterranean diet were 50-70% less likely to experience any kind of cardiac ailments. Since olive oil was specifically recommended in this study for it's monounsaturated fat content, these results are where the belief that olive oil is healthy originated.

But what we don't hear about the Lyon Diet Heart Study is this important fact: Fully 25% of the people on the Mediterranean diet either died or experienced a new cardiac event during the four-year study. That's one in four people on the Mediterranean diet! From this vantage point, these results don't look so good after all. They tell us that switching from saturated to monounsaturated fat is probably a good idea, but that the Mediterranean Diet will still leave you with considerable risk to your heart.

Compare these results to Dr. Caldwell Esselstyn's diet, which is vegan with no oil or other fats included. The patients in this study had suffered from an average of three cardiac events before the study started – they were truly, in most cases, on death's door. Among all of his patients that fully adhered to his diet, there was not one further cardiac event in twelve years. His suggested total fat intake? Less than 10%.[111]

In further proof, here's another compelling study from the University of Maryland: A group of students' arteries were tested after eating a 900-calorie breakfast, to see the effects of fat on the blood vessels' ability to expand and contract. (Blood vessels need to be able to expand and contract to regulate blood flow to the organs that need it most.) Half of the students had a fat free breakfast of 900 calories, and the other half had a fatty breakfast of 900 calories. After breakfast, the student's were tested to see how quickly their arteries could bounce back after being restricted for five minutes. The arteries of the group that had no fat in their breakfast bounced back quickly after being constricted for five minutes, but the arteries of the group that had the fatty breakfast took up to six hours to regain their ability to expand and contract normally.[112]

If you're still not convinced that olive oil is unhealthy, here are some more results to ponder: The same researchers at the University of Maryland found that eating bread dipped in olive oil reduced the arteries' ability to dilate by 31%.[113] This suggests a temporary reduction in the ability of the lining of the blood vessels to produce nitric oxide, which stimulates the vessels to dilate so blood can travel through them more easily.

While the old conventional wisdom was that a diet of 30% fat was healthy, these data suggest that a fat intake anywhere near 30% – even if it's from "healthy" monounsaturated fat – is probably far too high if you want to avoid heart disease.

So where do dairy and egg products fit in to this story? Dairy and egg products are notorious for their fat content, and as we've just seen, a fatty diet is highly linked to heart disease.

For all of you still convinced that eggs can't possibly be bad for us – they are the perfect protein after all – take note of these sobering statistics:

- The Physician's Health Study found that there was a 23% increase in the risk of death in people who ate just one egg a day.[114]

- Just 3-4 eggs a week has been linked with an increase in heart disease[115] – many people can eat that in one day!

- In a large analysis of 14 studies, researchers found that people who ate the most eggs had a 19% increased risk for developing heart disease compared with those who ate the fewest eggs.[116]

Non-Fat Dairy

Many people choose low-fat or non-fat dairy products in an attempt to eat a healthier diet. For your heart, that's a good step: A full quarter of Americans' fat intake comes from dairy products. However, when you switch from full-fat to non-fat dairy, the fat content is decreased but the protein content is increased. (Figure 4.3) As we've already discussed, animal protein is highly linked to cancer. So, it could be argued that if you eat low fat dairy you are putting yourself at risk of cancer (39% of calories from protein), and if you eat high fat dairy you put yourself at risk of both cancer (27% of calories from protein) and heart disease (35% of calories from fat) – neither of which are good options.

On a side note, when fat is taken out of dairy products, not only is the protein content increased, but the sugar content is also increased. Lactose sugar contributes more than 55% of skim milk's calories, giving it a calorie load similar to soda.[117]

**Figure 4.3: Percentages of Calories from
Fat and Protein in 2% Milk, Skim Milk and Non-Fat Milk**

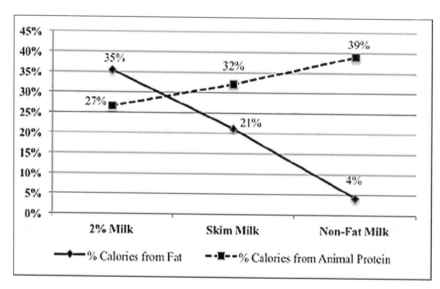

Unfortunately, dairy products don't just increase your risk for heart disease and cancer, they are also, believe it or not, bad for your bones…

DAIRY AND OSTEOPOROSIS

We have all heard about osteoporosis, the disease that causes our bones to become brittle and prone to breaking with old age. It's easy to believe that if someone has osteoporosis they should simply be careful not to fall, and if they do fall, they will just get a cast and it will heal like other people's broken bones. Unfortunately, it's not that simple. Osteoporosis is a devastating disease that is associated with a very high rate of morbidity and mortality.

Our bones are constantly in a state of both deterioration and renewal; they are continually breaking down and rebuilding themselves throughout our lives (much like our hair, which both falls out and simultaneously grows back in throughout our lives.) When we are young, our bones rebuild themselves faster than they break down, so our bones are becoming stronger during our younger years; after about the age of 30, our bones break down more quickly than they rebuild, which makes them become weaker as we age.

Osteoporosis occurs in elderly people because the bones have broken down to the point where they have become brittle, like a very dry leaf that's fallen off a tree. If an elderly person with osteoporosis breaks a bone, the bone is likely to take months to heal – if it fully heals at all – because this process of rebuilding bone has become so slow and ineffective. A broken leg on a child might heal in weeks; a broken leg on an osteoporotic person will likely take months to heal, if it ever fully heals at all.

While it is hard to imagine being elderly if you're still in the prime of your life, we have to remember that older people simply aren't as nimble as they were in their younger years. They fall because they are less steady on their feet, can't see where they are going as well, and are more likely to lose their balance. Furthermore, they have less strength and a slower reaction time to stop themselves from falling once they do start to fall.

Osteoporosis is a very debilitating disease. A person with osteoporosis can break one of her vertebrae simply by stepping off a curb. The slight drop down from the sidewalk to the street can cause enough impact on a vertebrae to fracture it! That's how brittle bones can become with osteoporosis. It's not uncommon for a person to have many fractured vertebrae at the same time, leaving the person with incredible chronic back pain.

Earlier on in the disease, smaller bones are more likely to break, but as a person's bones become more and more brittle, larger bones like hip bones become a very common site for breaks. Because our bones take longer and longer to rebuild as we age, the larger the bones that break, the less likely the person is to recover. In fact, 13.5% of people who fall and break a hip die within 6 months.[118] Fifteen percent (15%) of women in the U.S. will have a hip fracture in her lifetime. An estimated 10 million Americans have osteoporosis, and another 34 million have low bone mass, placing them at increased risk for osteoporosis.[119]

How do we avoid developing osteoporosis in our later years? Most people believe the answer is to eat dairy products for their calcium. We've all been taught that dairy = calcium and that calcium = strong bones, so one can surmise that dairy products = strong bones, right? Aren't we all taught at a very young age that "milk does a body good?" If we just make sure we are eating enough dairy products, then we should be able to avoid osteoporosis. In fact, much research shows the exact opposite is true...

It is true that calcium makes up a large component of our bones, and it is true that dairy products have a lot of calcium in them. However, dairy products come with a high concentration of animal protein, and the amino acids found in animal protein (but not plant protein) create by-products when they are metabolized, which creates an acidic environment in our blood and urine.

Here is why this is important: Our blood needs to maintain a very narrow pH level. If your blood becomes too basic or acidic you will die very quickly. Fortunately, the body is adept at recognizing that our blood pH levels are at jeopardy of being out of the normal range, and can quickly self correct when this happens.

How the body self-corrects for acidic pH is very important: When our blood becomes too acidic, such as after a meal laden with dairy products, the body lowers the acidity in the bloodstream by leaching calcium out of our bone marrow to act as a buffer, and thus protect the body by creating a more basic (less acidic) environment. Many researchers now believe that when we drink a glass of milk (or eat dairy products in general, which all start as milk), our bodies take more calcium out of our bones to help decrease the acidity in our blood than we ingested through the glass of milk in the first place. The result is a net deficit of calcium in the bones.

You may be scratching your head right now, thinking, "If this were really true, wouldn't all the high dairy-eating societies have high rates of osteoporosis?" In fact, this is correct: Countries across the world that have the highest intake of calcium per person through dairy products are also the countries with the highest rates of osteoporosis.[120,121] (Figure 4.4) Harvard professor Mark Hegsted concluded

Figure 4.4: Animal Protein and Hip Fracture Rates

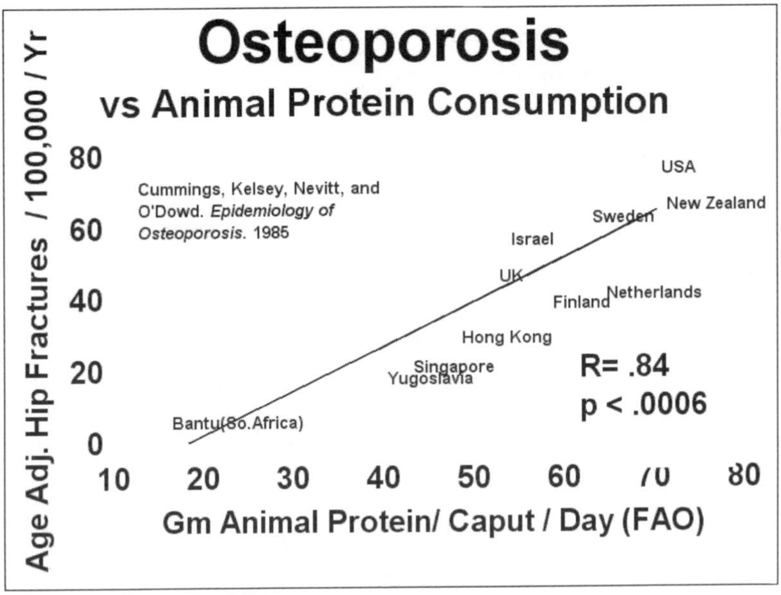

Source: Bill Harris, MD

91

in his paper on calcium and osteoporosis, "...hip fractures are more frequent in populations where dairy products are commonly consumed and calcium intakes are relatively high."[122]

Large-scale studies corroborate these results:

- In a 12-year Harvard study of 78,000 women, those who drank milk three times a day actually broke more bones than women who rarely drank milk.[123]
- In a study comparing dairy consumption to hip fractures, researchers showed that those with the highest dairy product consumption had approximately double the risk of hip fracture compared to those with the lowest consumption.[124]
- In a study of over 1,000 women, researchers showed that those with the highest animal protein to plant protein ratio had 3.7 times the rate of bone fractures than the women with the lowest ratios.[125]

To be fair, not all the large scale studies showed that dairy consumption puts you at a higher risk for bone fractures. In one study, Harvard researchers found that people who drank one glass of milk (or less) per week had a similar risk of breaking a hip or forearm than those who drank two or more glasses per week.[126,127]

So we have some studies showing that milk doesn't harm bones and some studies showing that it does harm bones. Here's what many of us want to know: If milk "does a body good," where are the large-scale, well- controlled studies that show that milk *protects* bones? That it helps *decrease* rates of bone fractures? The milk industry has nearly all of us believing with certainty that milk is good for our bones, but there seems to be virtually no strong evidence of that in the medical literature, and plenty of evidence supporting that milk is bad for our bones. Perhaps we shouldn't believe everything we're told: Milk may not do a body good after all.

DAIRY AND MULTIPLE SCLEROSIS

Like osteoporosis, there are several other diseases that have been linked to dairy consumption that you may not guess would be related. Multiple Sclerosis (MS) – an autoimmune disease – is one of them.

If you're not too familiar with autoimmune diseases, the easiest way to understand them is that they occur when the body mistakenly turns on itself and starts to attack its own cells. Our immune system is set up to attack anything that invades our bodies that shouldn't be there. For example, when you get a bacterial infection, your body recognizes the bacteria as invaders (antigens) which don't belong in your body, and your immune system mobilizes antibodies to mount an attack on them, killing them off so that you can be healthy again. It is, perhaps, the most amazing system in the body.

In an autoimmune disease, however, the body mistakenly identifies good protein or cells in a person's healthy tissue as invaders, and then attacks that healthy tissue in the body. In rheumatoid arthritis, for example, the body mistakenly attacks the protein in the joints, causing painful joints. In Type I Diabetes, the body mistakenly attacks the beta cells in the pancreas, leaving the pancreas unable to make insulin. In Multiple Sclerosis, the body mistakenly attacks the myelin sheath that protects nerve fibers, making the nerves unable to transmit signals throughout the body.

Our nerve fibers transmit electrical signals throughout the body, which, for example, let our brain signal to our legs to jump when we come upon a puddle, or to pull our fingers away when we've just touched a hot stove. Nerves let us feel sensation, like a hot stove or a fluffy dog, and our optic nerve gives us the sensation of sight. Nerves serve so many areas of the body that when a person develops MS, the entire body can eventually become affected. Many types of symptoms start to appear: fingers and toes go numb or tingly, it becomes difficult to walk without stumbling, and the person can go blind. In advanced cases, the person simply loses all feeling in his or her body, and be unable to move at all.

So why do researchers think that the body is turning on itself in the case of MS? There are many theories, but one particularly compelling theory has gained a lot of followers, and that theory has to do with diet.

Researchers have noted for decades that MS tends to happen in higher latitudes around the world where the climate is cooler; MS is not very common in hot countries near the equator, for example, so many people assume MS is related to the weather and even move to a warmer climate after their initial diagnosis. MS is also more common in industrialized countries as opposed to poorer regions. But a very forward-thinking physician started noticing something interesting when he looked into MS findings a little bit deeper.

In the 1940's, Roy Swank, MD, was studying MS in Norway – an area where the prevalence of MS was relatively high compared to other parts of the world. He noticed something interesting when he looked at where the highest prevalence rates were in Norway: The people who lived along the coasts of Norway were getting MS at much lower rates than people living inland. When he started hypothesizing why this may be, he noticed a difference in their diets: Norwegians living on the coasts tended to eat more fish, while those living inland tended to eat more dairy products.

One theory that has come from this observation is that fish or fish oil may be protective against MS symptoms. In fact, there is some research that shows that this may be true. But Dr. Swank didn't think that was the full story – he hypothesized that the difference in MS rates might be due to the levels of saturated fats between the two diets. The inlanders who ate more dairy products had a much higher intake of saturated fat in their diets.

After moving to the states, Dr. Swank took this hypothesis and began one of the more profound studies ever published in diet and disease. He studied 144 people for 35 years, dividing them up into two groups – those eating a regular (high saturated fat) diet, and those eating a very low saturated fat diet (under 20g of fat per day.) Since almost all saturated fat comes from animal foods, patients in his studies were cutting out or cutting way down on most animal based foods.

What he found over 35 years is absolutely astounding: *After 35 years, only 5% of the patients who ate the low fat diet were dead, while 80% of those who at the high fat diet were dead.* Furthermore, the 95%

of the low fat group that were still alive were only mildly disabled.[128] This is a very rare outcome for patients with MS. People who have had MS for 35 years are generally very disabled or dead. No drug for MS has ever shown such positive results.

Since the time when Dr. Swank's studies were published, researchers have looked further into this question. Is it any saturated fat that causes a problem, or just saturated fat from animals? What if it is not the fat causing the disease, but animal protein, as is now thought to be the case with many cancers? This research question is still being studied, but there is some early evidence that dairy products are highly correlated with MS.

For example, researchers in Canada found that there was nearly a 200% increase in the risk of MS in people who ate 33g of animal fat above baseline amounts.[129] They also found a significant protective effect against MS with higher intakes of vegetable protein, dietary fiber, cereal fiber, vitamin C, thiamin, riboflavin, calcium and potassium – all things found in high amounts in plant foods, but not in animal foods.

Researchers in France hypothesized that there is a factor in cow's milk that, in some people, triggers a latent virus to become active and cause MS. They studied the correlation between milk consumption and MS in 27 countries and 29 different populations. They found a strong correlation of 83.6% between milk consumption and the prevalence of MS, a correlation of 61.9% between cream consumption and the prevalence of MS, and a correlation of 50.4% between the consumption of butter and MS.[130] (Figure 4.5) There was no correlation between cheese and MS prevalence. The fact that the correlation, while still significant, was less with cream and butter and that there was no correlation with cheese suggest that liquid cow's milk contains factor(s) that could trigger a latent virus that may no longer be present when the milk has been processed into by-products.

Another interesting point that came out of this same study is that while MS is associated with latitude, as mentioned earlier, milk consumption was correlated even higher with latitude; countries in higher latitudes tend to eat more dairy products. Furthermore, if you

**Figure 4.5: Milk Consumption and the
Prevalence of Multiple Sclerosis**

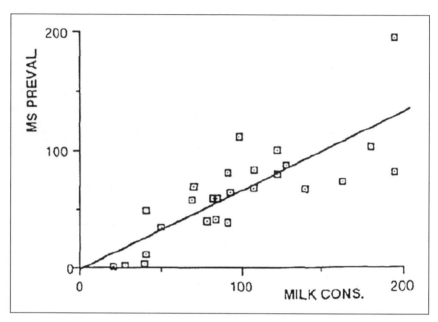

Source: Malosse D, Perron H, Sasco A, et al. *Correlation between milk and dairy product consumption and multiple sclerosis prevalence: a worldwide study.* Neuroepidemiology 11 (1992): 304-312.

look at countries in the same latitude that have very different intakes of dairy, like Japan (less dairy) and Greece (more dairy), they also have very different rates of MS (Japan 3.8 cases per 100,000, Greece, 35 cases per 100,000.) So, perhaps a person's latitude has little or nothing to do with MS – it's just that people in higher latitudes tend to eat more dairy products.

Even though we may not know if dairy products actually cause MS, they are undoubtedly correlated with MS in a strong way.

[Note: While Dr. Swank's data showed that a very low-fat diet worked in staving off the effects of MS, this was only true when their MS was not very advanced. When the disease was advanced and the patients had already deteriorated greatly, the patients did not experience renewed health. Therefore, it is extremely important that newly diagnosed MS patients be told of these data so that they can make important changes to their diet early in life … and hopefully enjoy a happy, healthy and long life.]

DAIRY AND DIABETES

Now that we've discussed MS, let's turn to another disease that has incredible research linking its prevalence to dairy products – Diabetes. You have certainly heard of diabetes, and if you don't have it yourself, you definitely know someone who does. Diabetes occurs when the beta cells in the pancreas do not produce enough insulin to keep our blood sugar levels normal.

Diabetes is a terrible disease because it causes inflammation that affects almost every organ in the body. Most notably, diabetes causes blood vessels throughout the body to get clogged up. When large vessels in the body are clogged it causes an alarmingly high rate of heart disease and stroke; when small vessels in the body are clogged, it causes blindness, kidney failure and neuropathies. Because of this, diabetes is the number one cause of blindness in working-age adults, the number one cause of kidney failure, and also the number one cause of non-accident amputation in the U.S.

There are two types of diabetes – Type I diabetes and Type II diabetes. The kind of diabetes we hear about most often is Type II diabetes because it affects 90-95% of all diabetics. Generally, in Type II diabetes, a person's bad diet overburdens their pancreas, which tries to produce more and more insulin to keep their blood glucose levels normal. Eventually, the pancreas gets tired and basically collapses in exhaustion. The pancreas ends up either not working very well, or not working at all. Type II diabetes is almost always associated with a high-fat, high-cholesterol diet. As we've discussed, eggs are loaded with fat and cholesterol, and one study found that diabetic patients had a 5-fold greater risk of cardiovascular death by eating 1 egg a day or more.[131] Another group of studies found that those who ate the most eggs had a 68% increased risk for developing diabetes compared with those who ate the fewest eggs; if they already had diabetes, their risk of developing heart disease jumped by 83%.[132]

Doctors like Joel Fuhrman, MD, John McDougall, MD and Neal Barnard, MD have shown that Type II diabetes is absolutely reversible in most people if they switch to a low-fat, plant-based diet. In a 22 week study comparing patients on a low-fat vegan diet versus the American Diabetes Association's (ADA) Recommended Diet, 43% of the vegan group, but only 26% of the ADA group, were able to reduce their diabetes medications; hemoglobin A1C fell 1.23 points in the vegan group, but only .38 points in the ADA group; LDL cholesterol fell 21.2% in the vegan group, but only 10.5% in the ADA group.[133] It's thought that a healthy, low-fat, plant-based diet probably gives the exhausted pancreas a much needed rest, and allows it to start working properly again with a little bit of time. So we know that Type II diabetes is generally linked to a diet high in fat[134] – such as a diet high in dairy and egg products – and can often be reversed. It is usually found in overweight people.

Let's turn to Type I diabetes, an autoimmune disease that is not currently curable, and affects 5-10% of diabetics. Type I diabetes is often referred to as juvenile diabetes because it typically strikes children while they are young. In Type I diabetes, the body mistakenly attacks the healthy beta cells in the pancreas and the beta cells quit producing insulin altogether. No one knows for sure why it happens, but there are a handful of popular theories.

One theory that is particularly compelling links Type I diabetes with drinking cow's milk at an early age: One study found that in 230 infants followed through 10 years of age, those who did not have cow's milk proteins were 60% less likely to develop Type I diabetes, compared with those who drank cow's milk formula during infancy.[135]

Why might this be? As it turns out, the protein found in cow's milk has an amino acid sequence that is very similar to the sequence found in the beta cells in the pancreas. It is hypothesized that some children's bodies reject cow's milk (which isn't surprising, as cow's milk is made for baby cows, not baby humans) and when the child's body begins to attack the protein from the cows milk, it also mistakenly attacks the beta cells in the pancreas at the same time, causing Type I diabetes. This theory is gaining a lot of momentum in the medical world, and parents are cautioned not to feed infants and young children cow's milk.

Sadly, Type I diabetes cannot be cured like Type II diabetes often can. Surprisingly, however, a low fat, plant based diet can help them reduce their need for insulin quite drastically: A researcher found that giving normal weight, Type I and Type II insulin dependent diabetics a strict, low-fat, nearly vegetarian diet for just three weeks had profound effects: Type I patients reduced their need for insulin by an average of 40%, and dropped their cholesterol by 30%. Furthermore, 24 of the 25 Type II patients were able to quit taking insulin altogether.[136] Since Type I diabetic patients make no insulin at all, doctors would not expect diet to have an effect on their level of insulin injections. Yet, this study shows just how powerful diet can be!

OTHER MALADIES RELATED TO DAIRY PRODUCTS

There are other health concerns that come with dairy products that aren't classified as diseases, but are still very real and can be troubling to the people who experience them. Two of them are lactose intolerance and cheese addiction.

Lactose Intolerance

Lactose is a sugar found in milk. When we are babies, we create the specific enzyme required to break down lactose so we can safely drink our mother's milk. However, when we turn about 2 years old, we generally stop producing that enzyme. This makes sense because, once we are weaned from our mothers, we simply don't need to drink milk anymore. Babies from just about every species of animal are weaned off their mother's milk after infancy or very early childhood.

When our bodies no longer create the enzyme needed to break down lactose, we can become intolerant to it. This explains why so many adults are lactose intolerant. It is actually normal for an adult to be lactose intolerant, because we are not designed to drink milk after we are weaned. Studies show that 75% of the world is lactose intolerant,[137] and it is particularly common in people of Asian, South American and African descent. About 25% of people of European descent are lactose intolerant. Lactose intolerance can cause:[138]

- Wheezing, asthma
- Rhinitis, runny nose
- Rashes, hives
- Abdominal pain
- Bloating
- Constipation
- Diarrhea
- Flatulence
- Iron-deficient anemia
- Itchy, swollen eyes

The fact that most adults are lactose intolerant is probably a sign that milk is not ideal for an adult body ... not human's milk or cow's milk.

Cheese Addiction

Nutrition researchers are starting to notice that some foods – like cheese and sugar – actually have addictive properties. Since vegetarians often say the main reason they can't go vegan is because they can't give up cheese, let's find out what the research says about this.

In 1981 researchers found that cow's milk has both morphine and casomorphins in it. Morphine is a powerful opiate drug usually given to people in the hospital to lessen pain and produce a calming effect. Morphine is highly addictive and is thus a controlled substance by the government. The morphine found in milk (both cow's and human's milk!) is in small amounts, but it is definitely there. It is hypothesized that morphine is found in milk to produce a calming effect on babies, thus helping babies to bond with their mothers when nursing.

Casomorphins are also found in cow's milk. Casomorphins start as casein, a protein that we have talked about in depth, which is found in high quantities in cow's milk (but low quantities in human milk.) It turns out that casein breaks apart during digestion and releases a host of opiates into our systems, called casomorphins. One type of casomorphin found in cow's milk has the pain-killing potency of about 1/10th the dose of morphine.[139]

Therefore, when we eat dairy products – and especially cheese, which has a high concentration of casein – it is very possible that we can have a subtle calming experience, as if we have just taken a low dose of drugs. No wonder people "just can't seem to give up cheese!"

DAIRY AND CHEMICALS

While it's important to rely on research to make good decisions, there are simply some things that we probably will never be able to prove. For example, we will probably never have large-scale proof from medical studies that chemicals in our food cause disease. This is because people eat and breathe in so many things in through their mouths every day that it would be next to impossible to prove that one specific chemical sprayed on crops, for example, is the culprit behind disease, when we are ingesting thousands of chemicals through our food and air. It's just too difficult to prove. So, sometimes it is necessary to use good common sense.

If you look at our food supply, we know that there are trace amounts of all sorts of chemicals in most of our food, usually put there by spraying chemicals on our crops or feeding hormones, antibiotics and chemical laden feed to our cattle and chickens. We are told by the FDA that these trace amounts have been studied in animals and are safe.

However, how can the FDA really be sure these chemicals are safe? First of all, humans are not animals, and scientists know that less than half of the studies done in animals have outcomes that are applicable to humans. Furthermore, even if it's true that eating a trace amount of Chemical X every day won't cause harm, the average American probably eats far more than just a trace amount of Chemical X ... and they are eating dozens of other chemicals as well. Interestingly, the FDA once told us that DDT (among many other chemicals) was completely safe, and they were definitely wrong about that.

A scary statistic from The Journal of Agricultural and Food Chemistry reports that there are up to 20 different pharmacologically active chemicals found in milk alone.[140] Since all dairy products start as milk, this statistic should generally hold true for cheese, yogurt, ice cream, butter and all other dairy products as well.

Look at these lists of chemicals found in milk and some of their known effects on human health, and ask yourself if this is what you want to put in your body, and in the bodies of your loved ones:[141]

Chemicals Found in Milk:

• Benezene	• Hexachlorobenzene
• Benzene	• Lindane
• Bromodichloromethan	• Permethrin
• Chlorobenzene	• Styrene
• Chloroform	• Tetrachloroethylene
• Chlordane	• Trans
• DDE	• Trichloroethylene
• Dioxin	• Toluene
• Dieldrin	• Xylene
• Endosulfan Sulfate	• 1,1,1-Trichloroethane
• Heptachlor Epoxide	• 2,4-Trimethylbenzene
• Heptachlor	

Many of these chemicals are known to have effects on humans. For example, DDE has been associated with cancer, liver failure, endocrine disruption, developmental disorders and a shortened lactation in nursing women. Dioxins have been associated with cancer, altered immune function, central nervous system disorders, liver function disruption, kidney function disruption, reduced fertility, endometriosis, endocrine disruption and developmental disorders.[142]

Chemicals are not natural for the human body. Pesticides, for example, are neurotoxins – their sole job is to kill the nervous system of insects. Knowing this, one can't help but wonder what these chemicals are doing to *our* nervous systems? Trace amounts add up, and many of these chemicals take years – even decades – to leave our bodies.

So what do we do with this information? We use our common sense. Look at the rates of disease over the past century. The incidence of certain diseases, like heart attacks and Type II diabetes, can be directly linked to poor diet and lack of exercise, but the incidence of autism, asthma, allergies, cancer, ADHD, learning disorders, psychiatric disorders, Alzheimer's disease and many other health problems has multiplied exponentially over the past few decades without an obvious cause. Ironically – or maybe not – much of this increase coincides with the use of chemicals in our food supply. While we may never know for sure, why gamble your health and the health of your loved ones? It's a good idea to not only eliminate dairy and eggs from your diet, but also buy organic as much as possible.

"Change the changeable,
accept the unchangeable,
and remove yourself from
the unacceptable."
– Denis Waitley

Chapter 5

DAIRY, EGGS AND OUR ENVIRONMENT

"The Environment" can seem like an overwhelming topic that people can't do much to change on their own; many people think that protecting the environment is a topic for the large corporations that create mass-scale pollution, and the governments that regulate them. However, there is a lot we can do on an individual level that will make a difference, as you'll read in the coming pages.

While the challenges facing our environment are getting more and more coverage in the press, they can still be hard to fully understand. We hear a lot about global warming, and that our planet is heating up. We hear that our air is polluted. We hear that we are running out of fresh water, and that what we have left is becoming extremely polluted. We hear that the world's forests are getting cut down at the rate of hundreds of acres per day. We hear that weather disasters like hurricanes, droughts and storms are becoming more common and more severe. But why are these issues more of a problem now than in previous generations? And what is causing them?

Many environmental organizations are pointing their fingers directly at the food industry, and especially to the factory farming and agricultural methods that have become so pervasive over the past fifty years. In a groundbreaking report called *Livestock's Long Shadow*, The United Nation's Food and Agriculture Organization concludes, "The livestock sector emerges as one of the top two or three most significant contributors to the most serious environmental problems at every scale from global to local."[143]

Yet few people even know that what we chose to eat has anything at all to do with the environment. Most people don't know how raising a cow for its beef or dairy products increases global warming, or how raising a chicken for its meat or eggs causes billions of fish to die in our waterways.

Indeed, raising animals for food is one of the most damaging things we can do to our environment, as you'll read in the coming pages. As a vegetarian, if you are already aware that raising cattle and pigs for their meat has huge environmental implications, you may not realize just how bad the dairy and egg industries are as well.

Some environmental reports that separate out the damage done by raising animals for meat versus those raised for their dairy and egg products show that the dairy and egg industries are often leading the destruction. Dairy farms and egg factories have a bigger effect on certain environmental catastrophes than even the meat industry does, as we'll discuss shortly. Furthermore, dairy cows and laying hens are in the factory farming system much longer than animals raised for their meat, so they have a far more damaging effect per animal on our environment.

As a vegetarian, you are already making a big difference to our environment by not supporting the meat and fishing industries, but you need to know that the dairy and egg industries are also a major contributing factor to all of the main environmental concerns. Let's talk about what is wrong with our air, water and land, what the dairy and egg industries have to do with it, and how we can make a difference to our environment every single day, with every mouthful we choose to eat.

AIR & CLIMATE
Air Temperature: Global Warming
Everyone has heard about global warming. It is now an undisputed fact among scientists that not only is our planet heating up, it's heating up at the fastest rate in recorded history. But is this really a problem? When we hear that the estimated increase is 2°F - 11.5°F,[144] we wonder how bad can that really be? It doesn't sound like that much.

Although 2° - 11.5°F doesn't sound like much, the truth is that even a small temperature increase can cause incredible damage. Here are just a handful of examples, many of which are already happening:

- Rising temperatures are causing glaciers around the North Pole to melt off rapidly. Huge areas of glaciers – the size of U.S. states – are breaking off from the artic pole and melting in the water. Between 1965 and 2000, the ocean ice thinned by 40% in the arctic.[145] Here are some of the consequences of melting glaciers:

  ▫ Melting glaciers are threatening the world's polar bear population. Polar bears are dying off because they use the ice floes as little islands to rest when they swim for food. Due to global warming, many ice floes are melting and disappearing. With fewer ice floes, the polar bears have to swim further and further to find food. Sometimes they don't find food at all because it has become too far away, and they starve. Other times they drown from exhaustion as they cannot find an ice floe to rest on when are out in the ocean.

  ▫ Melting glaciers are raising the level of the oceans around the world. By 2100, the mean sea level is expected to rise by about 3.5" – 34.6".[146] There are some island nations, like the Maldives, that are literally expected to be underwater in a matter of decades.

  ▫ Melting glaciers threaten our fresh water supply. In some places, the seawater is rising up over fresh groundwater aquifers, causing the fresh water to become salty due to salt water intrusion. In these cases, there will be little or no fresh water for people or animals in those areas.

  ▫ Melting glaciers are ruining beaches and properties. Some beaches where families have gone for years to vacation are now at risk of going underwater, and peoples' homes and properties are also at risk of being permanently flooded. When coastal properties are permanently flooded, real estate values drop dramatically, negatively affecting the local economy.

- Rising temperatures are changing weather patterns all over the world. Many meteorologists have noted changing weather patterns around the world that are much more severe than in previous decades: Droughts, floods, hurricanes, tornadoes and other natural disasters have been much more frequent and far more severe in recent decades as the planet is heating up. The United States had its hottest July in recorded history in 2012, which was accompanied by an extremely severe drought in the Midwestern states that sharply increased the price of food. Many weather experts are now arguing that these natural disasters aren't really "natural" at all – they are a result of global warming affecting weather patterns.

  ◻ Some regions will experience heat waves and droughts, rendering many countries that already suffer from drought and starvation even more susceptible to the lack of waterfall.

  ◻ Other regions will experience extremely increased rainfall, due to increased evaporation from the hotter temperatures.

  The results will likely be that thousands or millions of people will die, starve, become ill, homeless, orphaned or befall other tragedies.

- Rising temperatures can kill off entire ecosystems, which are delicately balanced on temperature and other factors. Some animal, fish and plant species cannot survive if their habitat increases in temperature by even two degrees, and many are expected to become extinct as a result of global warming. Tundra, mangroves and coral reefs are expected to be particularly vulnerable to global warming.

  ◻ The United Nations reports, "One-third of all amphibians, a fifth of mammals and an eight of all birds are now threatened by extinction [due to habitat loss, exploitation and climate change.]"[147]

- Rising temperatures allow some types of pests to flourish. In Alaska, pests that thrive in the warmer climate are now destroying some of the great conifer forests.

- Rising temperatures will make it harder to grow food in certain parts of the world. It is estimated that by 2030, maize production in South Africa could reduce by 30% due to global warming, while rice, millet and maize could decrease by 10% in Southeast Asia.[148] As the world's population continues to boom, this could put many people at risk of malnutrition or starvation.

Now that we understand just how serious global warming is, let's turn our attention to what causes it, and, in particular, what factory farming's role is in this environmental catastrophe.

Greenhouse Gasses

Our planet's atmosphere is crucial for life on Earth: Among many things, our atmosphere regulates the air we breathe, controls the Earth's temperature, provides water and protects us from harmful radiation. The atmosphere contains many elements, but certain elements can absorb and emit infrared radiation. This helps to trap heat in our atmosphere, keeping our planet warm – just like a greenhouse. Therefore, these gasses that help trap heat in our atmosphere are called "greenhouse gasses" and are noted for their role in keeping our planet warm. Without greenhouse gasses, it is estimated that our plant would be 59°F cooler.

The main greenhouse gasses are water vapor, carbon dioxide, methane, ozone, nitrous oxide and chloroflourocarbons. You can see in table 5.1 the estimated effect of the four major gasses on our greenhouse effect.[149,150,151]

Scientists around the world agree that we humans have been increasing the levels of greenhouse gasses through human activity, resulting in an increased temperature on our planet's surface of about 1.4°F warmer than it was in the early part of the 20th century. It's estimated that about two thirds of that increase has happened

Table 5.1: The Four Major Greenhouse Gasses and Their Percentage of Contribution to the Greenhouse Effect

GAS	% OF GREENHOUSE EFFECT
Water Vapor	36-40%
Carbon Dioxide (CO2)	9-26%
Methane (CH4)	4-9%
Ozone (O3)	3-7%

since 1980.[152] Scientists vary on how much they estimate our planet will warm in the coming decades, but, again, the estimates range from 2°F – 11.5°F.[153] As noted earlier, because of varying weather patterns around the world, some parts of the world are expected to have higher increases in temperature than other areas, and some will experience less rainfall while other areas will experience much more.

Our Role in Increasing Greenhouse Gasses

How are we humans contributing to global warming? Anytime we engage in activities that increase greenhouse gas emissions, we contribute to global warming. One way we do this is by burning fossil fuels, such as petroleum, coal, and natural gas. When we burn fossil fuels, carbon dioxide is released into our atmosphere. Levels of carbon dioxide in our atmosphere are 100 ppm higher than they were in the pre-industrial era.[154] The main sources of fossil fuel burning that we hear about are transportation and industrial activities. This is why we are encouraged to carpool or bicycle to work, buy hybrid cars and turn our heat down in our homes. It is also why the government is pressured to continually restrict carbon dioxide emissions from different industrial sectors. Carbon dioxide emissions are our main source of increasing greenhouse gasses.

However, there are a lot of other greenhouse gasses that we contribute to that may not have as high of a percentage as carbon dioxide in the atmosphere, but have a more potent effect. Two of these gasses are methane and nitrous oxide. Methane is 24 times more potent than carbon dioxide, and is rising as a percentage in our atmosphere. Similarly, nitrous oxide is 296 times more potent than carbon dioxide. A very small increase in nitrous oxide in our atmosphere can have a very big effect.[155] Therefore, industries that emit carbon dioxide, methane and nitrous oxide are big factors in warming our planet.

Another way that we increase global warming comes from cutting down trees and plants, which are nature's natural carbon dioxide recyclers. In the process of photosynthesis, trees and plants recycle and regulate carbon dioxide in our atmosphere. The more trees and plants we have, the lower the levels of carbon dioxide in our atmosphere; the more we cut down trees and plants, the higher the levels of carbon dioxide in our atmosphere. Therefore, when we cut down trees and plants, we inadvertently increase carbon dioxide in our atmosphere and contribute to global warming.

So how do the dairy and egg industries contribute to global warming? They contribute in a multitude of ways, including deforestation (cutting down millions of acres of forest around the world), daily operations that use electricity, diesel and other industrial energy sources, transportation, and through the massive amounts of manure and gaseous emissions the animals make, among other ways. Let's discuss these.

Deforestation

One of the main ways that the dairy and eggs industries contribute to global warming is through deforestation, or cutting down the Earth's forests. As previously discussed, when we cut down trees we reduce our planet's ability to recycle and regulate carbon dioxide in the atmosphere, which results in rising temperatures.

Why are we cutting down trees around the world for dairy and egg factory farms? The answer is to grow millions of acres of feed for dairy cows and laying hens. According to the United Nations, "The livestock sector accounts for 9% of anthropogenic [human-related] carbon dioxide emissions. The largest share of this derives from land-use changes – especially deforestation – caused by expansion of pastures and arable land for feed crops."[156] Livestock-induced emissions from deforestation are about 2.4 billion tons of carbon dioxide per year.[157] This really puts into perspective just how much land is being deforested for the livestock industry – whether it is by providing land for cattle to live, or for growing the copious amounts of feed that they eat.

The Amazon rainforest, in particular, gets a lot of press because of the astonishing rate at which it is getting cut down, the resulting loss of biodiversity and the rainforest's supreme importance to our atmosphere. The Amazon rainforest is considered to be one of the world's most diverse sources of insects, birds and wildlife, and is also a major force in regulating our atmosphere. However, it is getting cut down at the rate of hundreds of square miles a month to make room for beef cattle to graze and to grow grain and soy to feed cows and chickens in our factory farms.

This isn't just happening in the Amazon: About 260 million acres of forests in the U.S. have also been cut down to grow crops, and many millions more are being cut down around the world.[158] According to the United Nations, about 30% of the earth's ice-free land is directly or indirectly involved in the production of livestock,[159] and 70% of previous forested land in the Amazon is occupied by pastures, with feed crops covering most of the remainder.[160]

In addition to being a major contributing factor to global warming, deforestation is also the cause of extinction for many species. Different types of plants, animals, birds, insects and fish are found in very specific places on the planet, so when we decimate large areas of land, we can cause hundreds of species to become extinct. When we clear cut an entire section of Amazon rainforest, we cause extinction of certain plants and creatures (especially insects) that make that little area of the world their home.

Daily Operations & Transportation
In addition to deforestation, the dairy and egg industries increase the carbon dioxide in our atmosphere through their daily operations.

Fossil fuel that is used in manufacturing fertilizer, running factory farms and transporting animals and animal products are also major contributors to global warming. It is estimated that the carbon dioxide burned just to create the fertilizer used on crops for animal feed total over 41 million tons per year.[161] Fossil fuel burned through various energy sources to run factory farms may emit 90 million tons of carbon dioxide per year.[162] Dairy farms are especially high users of electricity (for refrigeration and processing), and their fossil fuel emissions used for electricity are even higher than their use for feed production.[163] Transporting livestock products is estimated to create just under a million tons of carbon dioxide emissions per year.[164] Compared with 1944, when dairy cows lived in more natural conditions on pastures as opposed to living in modern factory farms, carbon dioxide emissions have more than doubled per cow.[165]

Whether it's from burning fossil fuels to create fertilizer for the crops on the deforested land, or burning fossil fuels for the daily operations of the factory farms, we see that the dairy, egg and meat industries are major contributors to increased carbon dioxide in our atmosphere.

Manure and Gasseous Emissions

Cows, interestingly, emit methane through their manure, when they belch, when they are flatulent, and even when they breathe. Cows can be particularly gaseous because they are fed a poor diet of processed feed that is not natural for them. This poor quality feed significantly increases their gaseous emissions, which are particularly high in methane.

As previously mentioned, methane is 24 times more potent than carbon dioxide, so it is a big threat to our atmosphere.[166] If you're wondering just how much methane can be emitted through gaseous cows, listen to this statistic: *According to the Environmental Protection Agency (EPA), the world's livestock are responsible for 25% of methane emissions caused by human activity,[167] and animal agriculture produces 100 million tons of methane a year.[168] This is more than all the cars, trucks, planes and trains put together.* Chickens also contribute to this statistic, but not at the same rate as cows.

Nitrous oxide, which again, is 296 times more potent than carbon dioxide, is also a serious greenhouse gas created by factory farms. It primarily comes from cows' manure and the slurry pits on factory farms. Dairy farm generally have the largest slurry pits in the animal agriculture industry. The livestock sector is responsible for 65% of nitrous oxide from human activity, and current trends suggest this percentage is increasing substantially.[169]

To understand just how much the livestock sector affects global warming, let's finish the topic of global warming with some sobering statistics:

- Our atmosphere's concentrations of carbon dioxide and methane have increased by 36% and 148% respectively since 1750.[170]

- About 25% of the increase in carbon dioxide from human activity over the past two decades is caused mostly by changes in land-use, particularly deforestation.[171]

- The main greenhouse gases from livestock systems are methane from animals (25%), carbon dioxide from land use and its changes (32%), and nitrous oxide from manure and slurry (31%).[172]

- Finally, *According to the United Nations, 18% of the earth's greenhouse gas production is directly or indirectly attributable to the production of livestock – more than all transportation combined.*[173]

Interestingly, the World Bank's former lead environmental advisor wrote a very compelling article explaining why this last statistic from the UN is incorrect … and the correct percentage of greenhouse gas production due to livestock is closer to 51%.[174]

Air Quality

In addition to heating up our air and causing global warming, factory farms also impact our air quality, most dramatically on a local level in the communities where they reside. Factory farms release many volatile organic compounds into the air through their operations, including carbon monoxide, chloroflourocarbons, nitrogen oxide and sulphur dioxide.[175] Most of the air pollution, however, stems from the manure pits, which can take up acres on factory farms, and create an overwhelming stench that can be smelled from miles away. These manure pits create toxic levels of ammonia, methane, nitrous oxide, phosphorous and microbial pathogens in the air.

Accordingly, people who live near factory farms have associated health problems at very high rates not found in other communities. For example, 50% of children who live on or near a factory farm have asthma,[176] compared to the nation's average at 9.4%.[177] In Milford, Utah, where there is more manure waste than the entire state's human waste, the citizens have 20 times more diarrheal illness and 7 times more respiratory illness than citizens in other parts of the state.[178] Workers in the factory farms are highly susceptible to the fumes in the air (as are the animals themselves) and chicken and hen factories are anecdotally said to be the worst. The acidic stench around factory farms mainly comes the ammonia created from manure. Livestock create approximately 64% of the global ammonia emissions from human activities.[179]

These compounds in the air don't just affect air quality: When high amounts of gasses like sulphur dioxide and nitrogen dioxide react with moisture in the air, they are converted into acids which return to earth as acid rain and snow. They can also return as gas particles that damage crops, forests, lakes and streams, causing vast damage to plant and marine life.

Unfortunately, many people who live in rural areas lose nearly the entire value of their home when a factory farm opens up nearby. The stench from the manure pits is so overwhelming that many people wear masks when they go outside. Outdoor summer barbecues, family dinners on the deck and the laughter of playing children are mostly unheard of in communities near factory farms. Although many people may want to move after a factory farm opens in their community, most cannot, because they cannot find a buyer … not at any price.

WATER

Now that we understand the magnitude of the effect that factory farms have on our air temperature and air quality, let's turn to their role in our water supply and water quality.

It is shocking to learn just how scarce our fresh water is becoming and just how polluted our waterways have become. We may hear occasional reports about a local river being polluted or a dry summer causing a water shortage, but these topics never really seem to get much coverage in the media; it's quite shocking to learn the facts. Factory farms are a major cause of our water scarcity and water pollution problems. Upon understanding the issues and learning the facts, it is hard to turn a blind eye.

Water Scarcity

Many of us don't think about our water supply – we turn on our faucets and clean water comes out in abundance at any time of the day, in any quantity we want, hot or cold. We take long showers, run dishwashers, washing machines and sprinklers. We wash our bodies, dogs, cars, boats, RVs, windows, sidewalks, and porches. We water our gardens and trees and lawns. I expect most of us in developed countries take this for granted. Water has always been there when we wanted it, and it always will be. Or will it?

Fresh water is surprisingly scarce. Only 2.5% of all water resources on our planet are fresh water, and 70% of that is locked up in glaciers, permanent snow and the atmosphere.[180] Currently, 38% of the world's population lives in water stressed areas, and this is supposed to increase to 64% by 2025.[181]

If you're tempted to think that it's only the most arid countries in Africa that have true drought problems, you'll be surprised to learn that many industrialized countries are so short on water that laws have been inacted to force citizens to drastically cut back their water use. For example, citizens in certain areas of Australia are not allowed to hose off their sidewalk or other inorganic property, and are rationed on how often they can wash their cars.

It seems that Australia's situation may have been a foreshadowing for other countries. The United States experienced a summer drought in 2012 that was so severe that dozens of farms closed down permanently in the Midwest, and prices for corn, wheat, and other staples rose over 50% in just two months. That same summer, Russia experienced a similar drought, and Asia's monsoon rains were far lower than usual.

In further examples of water shortages, the island of Tuvalu literally ran down to only 3 days water supply after a long drought in 2011, and other island nations like the Maldives and Kiribati will likely lose their supply of fresh water as global warming raises the sea level which will cause salt water intrusion into their wells, spoiling their groundwater. Entire nations are facing the looming situation of not just having a reduced water supply, but having *no* water supply. That's how scarce water is becoming in some parts of the world.

What is happening to our fresh water? Where is it going? In some cases, there are droughts or the fresh water supply is spoiled through pollution or salt water intrusion. However, in other cases, we are simply using it all up.

Geologists have known for years that the United States has serious signs of diminished fresh water supply. Perhaps the scariest example comes from one of the largest fresh water sources in the world, the Ogallala Aquifer. Most of the middle states in the U.S. rely on the Ogallala Aquifer for their fresh water, including Texas, Nebraska, Colorado, Wyoming, Kansas, Oklahoma, New Mexico and South Dakota.

What, exactly, is an aquifer? An aquifer is a naturally made groundwater storage reservoir. Some aquifers –like the Ogallala – are fossil aquifers, which come from ancient glaciers that are now trapped deep underground as water.

While rainwater seeps through the ground to help refill many aquifers, they generally replenish at a very slow rate. Deep fossil aquifers – like the Ogallala – don't replenish much, if at all. Furthermore, dry states (like Colorado) have little rainfall and a lot of wind that evaporates the rain before it can seep down into the ground. These conditions hasten water renewal even further.

The Ogallala is one of the world's largest bodies of fresh water, providing about 30% of the total irrigation water for the U.S., and drinking water for 82% of the people who live in that region.[182] Until the 1950's, studies showed that the amount of water we were taking from the massive aquifer was so negligible that it was essentially undetectable. However, in the 1960's something began sucking the water out of the Ogallala at a very alarming rate: Factory farming.

Factory farming methods were invented in the mid 1900's, and factory farms began springing up all over the country, especially in the middle states, called "America's Heartland." As factory farming became more efficient, the numbers of animals increased exponentially, and now there are millions of concentrated animals living on these farms.

Factory farms use water for all kinds of reasons: Animals need water to drink, and the factories need water to clean their production units, wash animals, cool the facilities, and for waste disposal. The slaughterhouses also use massive amounts of water to clean out blood and waste, and throughout the meat extraction process. However, by far and away, the largest use of water in the livestock industry is in growing the massive quantities of feed given to the animals.

In factory farms, cows are mostly fed mass produced grain and chickens are mostly fed mass produced soy. Cows require 7 pounds of grain for every 1 pound of weight gain; chickens require 2 pounds of grain for every pound of weight gain.[183] It is in the growing of all this feed for livestock animals that so much of our water is being used. In fact, 70% of all arable land is dedicated to feedcrop production.[184]

All of these huge fields of grain and soy must be watered regularly, which one can witness from an airplane, flying over fields and seeing the watering systems that stretch as long as city blocks wheeling over the fields and spouting out thousands of gallons of water. Unfortunately, about 45% of the water sprayed on feed crops evaporates.[185] It takes 1,000 pounds of water to produce 1 pound of feed grain,[186] and it is estimated that irrigation alone accounts for almost

70% of worldwide fresh water use, with 15-35% of irrigation with-drawals being unsustainable.[187] By 2025, it's expected that water used for agricultural use will increase by 50% worldwide.[188]

While all types of animal farming require large amounts of water, it's argued that the dairy and egg industries require the most. Dairy cows require twice as much water a day as beef cows to service them, and laying hens require 50% more water than broiler hens.[189] Furthermore, lactating cows (dairy cows are almost always lactating) drink about 230% more than non-lactating cows.[190] Additionally, dairy cows and egg-laying hens live far longer than beef cattle or broiler chickens, respectively, so they eat a lot more food in their lifetime. The amount of grain grown just for the dairy and egg indus-tries – and the corresponding water used to grow it – is staggering. In fact, 70% of our grain does not go to feeding humans – it goes to feeding livestock whose products we eat.[191] Therefore, dairy cows and egg-laying hens are responsible for exponentially more water use per animal than cows and chickens raised for their meat.

Knowing that there are billions of animals in factory farms around the world, we can start to see how much water is used to bring animal products to our tables. Returning to the Ogallala

World Hunger

Many people point out that the world's hunger problem would be eradicated if we quit eating meat and instead fed all the grain currently going to feed livestock to the world's poor. They are correct. According to John Robbins in *The Food Revolution*, 1,400,000,000 people could be fed by the grain and soybeans eaten by U.S. livestock.[192]

Aquifer, we should not be surprised now to learn that we have been guzzling trillions of gallons of water from the Ogallala aquifer every year in order to water and grow grain for all of these animals we raise for meat, dairy and eggs. Sadly, while the Ogallala aquifer used to be flush with so much water it was seemingly endless, its water level is becoming shockingly low due to factory farming. In some parts of the aquifer, the water table drops by more than 5 feet per year (the aquifer runs from about 100 ft – 1,000 ft deep, depending on the location.) In some areas, especially further south, farmers have had to drill deeper wells to reach the declining water table, and in the Texas panhandle, the water table has been completely drained. Experts now estimate that only 10% of the water we use in the Ogallala aquifer is replenished each year, and some estimate it will run dry in as little as 25 years.

Sadly, this phenomenon is happening all around the world – not just in the Ogallla – as technology has created more powerful pumps that are sucking aquifers dry at faster and faster rates. Depletion of aquifers around the world has been cited as one of the causes of the "Great Food Crisis of 2011."[193] In an article in Time Magazine, author and editorial director of the WorldWatch Institute, Ed Ayres, notes, "Around the world, as more water is diverted to raising [cows], pigs and chickens, instead of producing crops for direct [human] consumption, millions of wells are going dry. India, China, North Africa and the United States are all running freshwater deficits, pumping more from their aquifers than rain can replenish."[194]

Water Pollution

In addition to using up all our fresh water, we are also destroying it with pollution. We humans dump garbage and sewage in our fresh water, run our boats and ships through it, and even dump our industrial waste in it. While most developed countries have laws in place designed to keep fresh water clean, one look at the Hudson River shows that the laws don't work nearly well enough. Furthermore, many countries around the world don't have strict laws about water pollution; in these countries, it is common practice for companies to

According to the United Nations, because dairy farming and growing feed for dairy cattle requires so much water, it takes 990 litres of water to produce one liter of milk.[195] Converting to ounces and gallons, we find:

One 8 ounce glass of milk requires approximately 62 gallons of water to produce.

dump industrial waste into the waterways, and for citizens to dump their sewage in it. In developing countries, 90-95% of public waste-water and 70% of industrial wastes are discharged into surface water without treatment.[196]

However, the number one source of fresh water pollution comes from factory farms – even in the U.S. where regulations are supposed to be tight. Dairy farms are known to be among the biggest contributors. Factory farming is making our waterways toxic through two major routes: Through fertilizers used in growing animal feed getting into our water, and through animal waste and drug residues getting into our water.

Fertilizer

Feeding billions of animals in factory farms requires growing billions of pounds of grain and soy products, as we've already discussed. The process of growing grain and soy almost always includes using massive amounts of fertilizer to make the grain grow faster and stronger. All this fertilizer goes onto the ground and much of it washes off the land into our rivers and streams. When fertilizer is sprayed on crops, it gets into our waterways through leaching, surface runoff, subsurface flow and soil erosion. Unbelievably, 40-60% of nitrogen (a main component in fertilizer) applied to crops is left in the soil or leached into waterways.[197] The fertilizer eventually ends up in our oceans, killing massive areas of marine life.

How does fertilizer that is sprayed on crops end up killing fish in the oceans? It happens when the nitrogen in fertilizer gets into our water. Fertilizer is very high in nitrogen. Fertilizer sprayed on crops runs off the land into our waterways. When nitrogen levels get too high in waterways, algae begins to grow out of control. This recruits bacteria, which feed on the algae, and the bacteria use up the oxygen in the water. If the bacteria level gets really high, this can eventually cause the water to become completely devoid of oxygen. Fish and other marine life need oxygen to survive, so when the oxygen in the water is gone, all marine life in that area suffocate and die. This whole process is called "eutrophication." An area that has no marine life due to eutrophication is called a "Dead Zone." (Figure 5.1.)

One of the most notable examples where this happens in the U.S. is the Mississippi River. There is a lot of farming around the Mississippi River, and the fertilizers used in that region run off the land into the river and get swept downstream into the Gulf of Mexico. The problem has become so bad that current estimates show a Dead Zone at the mouth of the Mississippi that is hundreds of square kilometers.

One Reason to Buy Organic Produce

Even vegans need to consider their impact on the environment. Conventional (non-organic) fruits and vegetables have almost always been treated with fertilizer to help the crops grow faster and bigger. Organic produce, on the other hand, has not been grown with synthetic (manufactured) fertilizers. By choosing organic produce you can avoid contributing to Dead Zones.

**Figure 5.1: How Fertilizing Crops Leads
to Dead Zones in our Waterways**

From Fertilizer to Dead Zone
Below is a quick schematic showing how fertilizing crops
kills millions of fish and other marine animals:

Fertilize crops
➔
Fertilizer, which has a lot of nitrogen in it, leeches off
the land and runs into waterways
➔
↑Nitrogen content in the Water
➔
↑Algae levels
➔
↑Bacteria
➔
↓Oxygen
➔
↓Ability for marine life to breathe
➔
Millions of fish, plankton, etc, suffocate to death
=
DEAD ZONE:
An area of water devoid of all life.

Sadly, this isn't just a problem in the U.S. – it's a global problem: There are areas along both North American coasts, Europe, South America, Australia as well as Asia that have very low concentrations of oxygen in the water.

Animal Waste and Drug Residues
As we've discussed, animals raised for food create a huge amount of manure. If one dairy farm has up to 18,000 dairy cows on it, and each

Manure Lagoons.
Manure from dairy factories is put into manure "lagoons,"
which can take up acres on a factory farm.

cow defecates several times a day, imagine how much manure piles up – literally! This is true of beef, pig, poultry, dairy and egg farms.

Once again, because dairy cows and egg laying hens live longer lives than cows and chickens raised for meat, they create far more waste per animal, making the dairy and egg industries the biggest culprits in the amount of manure created per animal.

What happens with all this manure? In a healthy ecosystem, manure is turned back to the crops as natural fertilizer. However, it is not feasible to take the enormous amounts of manure from millions of animals in factory farms and ship it around the country to return it to the land, so the majority of it is instead kept in manure pits. These manure pits are enormous, and one dairy factory farm will have many manure pits. One farmer described factory farms as "60 acres of concrete and 10 acres of manure pits."[198]

While manure is supposed to be contained in the manure pits, it sometimes gets out. A quick web search of "dairy manure spills" will lead to multiple articles:

- November 2012: "Dairy Blamed for Killing Fish with Manure Spill."
- June 2012: "Virginia Dairy Fined Nearly $12,000 for Manure Spill."

- May 2012: "A Timberville dairy producer has paid a $6,825 fine for allowing manure to spill into the North Fork of the Shenandoah River."
- April 2012: "Leak from OSU Dairy Research Center went into Oak Creek."
- December 2011: "An Arcadia dairy farmer is fined more than $7,200 for three manure spills that flowed into the Trempealeau River."
- April 2010: "Officials seek cause of Snohomish dairy-manure spill. Regulators are still trying to figure out what caused a dairy-farm lagoon to fail…"
- …And many, many more.

How does manure get out of the confinement containers? There are many ways. The containers can burst, leak or overflow (especially in heavy rains), the hoses can burst, pipes can burst, emergency shut-off valves can fail, or human error can occur. And when they do, the results are disastrous: The Sierra Club of Iowa noted one spill in March 2010 where a broken pipeline spilled manure at the rate of 800 gallons per minute, for a total leak of 50,000 – 70,000 gallons of manure.[199] In 1995, a hog farm in North Carolina spilled 25 million gallons of manure into the New River when a manure pit burst.[200] That is twice as much manure spilled into the New River as oil spilled by the Exxon-Valdez. They received a fine of $12.6 million dollars, equal to their gross sales over 10 hours.[201]

When these manure spills get into our rivers and waterways they become the cause of devastating fish kills. The reasons for this are two-fold: First, the bacteria in manure can cause devastating illnesses in fish that can kill them. This is an obvious source of contamination. Secondly, manure, like fertilizer, has nutrient and chemical properties (such as nitrogen, phosphorous and ammonia) that can deplete the oxygen in the water, and cause dead zones. When this happens, millions of fish die.

Nitrogen and phosphorous are considered the two biggest detriments to good water quality. Dairy and egg farms play a big role here: the phosphorous excreted by one cow is equal to that of 18-20 humans, and phosphorous content is highest in egg laying hens.[202] In one study, nitrogen concentration was found to be approximately 38 times higher around chicken factory farms than in forested areas.[203] Pesticide and herbicide use are also cited as contaminants to our environment. The United Nations says "the livestock sector is probably the leading contributor to water pollution by nitrogen and phosphorous in the United States."[204]

The EPA claims that agriculture (most of which goes toward livestock, as we've discussed) accounts for 75% of all water quality problems in the nation's rivers and streams,[205] and estimates that manure spills have polluted more than 35,000 miles of river.[206] Billions of fish have been killed in North Carolina alone.[207]

When our waterways are polluted by manure, it doesn't just affect the wildlife ... it can cause extensive human illness. The most notable is pfiesteria, a toxic microbe found in manure that can cause memory loss, severe cognitive impairment, kidney dysfunction, liver dysfunction, sores, burns, headaches, nausea, vomiting

Manure runoff from a dairy farm.
Government regulations don't stop environmental disasters. Manure spills are a regular occurrence, getting into our land, ground water and waterways.
Veganoutreach.org

and difficulty breathing. Other pathogens – some deadly – include campylobacter, E-Coli 0157:H7, Salmonella, clostridium botulinum, and giardia, just to name a few. These pathogens can also cause illness when polluted water is sprayed on crops, and the crops are then eaten.

In addition to contaminating our waterways, manure spills can leech into our groundwater as well. When this happens, people who get their drinking water from nearby shallow wells can become extremely ill. In 1993, Milwaukee's dairy manure leached into the ground water, and cryptosporidium from the manure sickened over 400,000 people and caused 100 deaths.[208] Residents of California and Wisconsin are at a particularly high risk of contaminated groundwater due to those states' thriving dairy industries. It is estimated that 65% of California's residents drink ground water that is threatened with contamination directly from the dairy farms.[209]

Finally, drug residues used in factory farms are also causing great damage to our water. Pharmaceuticals are used copiously in dairy and egg farms: Hormones and antibiotics are the most notable. Hormones are given to the animals to make them grow faster and produce more milk, so the farmers can make more money faster from the animals. Antibiotics are used to help ward off disease. We humans take antibiotics only when we are sick, but in the densely crowded factory farms, disease runs so rampant that farmers feed antibiotics to healthy animals in the hopes of preventing them from getting sick. The Institute of Medicine estimates that about 80% of the antibiotics administered to livestock in the U.S. are used in healthy animals to prevent disease.[210]

How are these drugs affecting our water? They actually show up in our waterways and in our drinking water! The animals excrete the drugs in their urine and feces, so when a manure spill occurs, these drugs actually end up in our waterways and our water supply.

The destruction that occurs with manure spills is far-reaching, and as pointed out previously, dairy farms are notorious for their spills. As consumers, we desperately want to believe that these events either don't happen or rarely happen. But in fact, they happen all the time.

Again, this is also not a problem confined to the U.S. It is happening all over the world, wherever there are large factory farm operations. Poultry farms in China, Thailand and Vietnam are polluting the South China Sea so badly that there are red tides, and the marine life is threatened.[211] Worryingly, as some of these extremely populated countries whose citizens traditionally couldn't afford much meat are getting wealthier – like China and India – they are eating exponentially more meat, dairy and egg products. Many environmentalists are concerned that our waterways simply won't hold up to the increasing demand for meat, dairy and egg products. They worry that many species of fish will become extinct and fresh water will become so scarce it won't support our population.

The United Nations report summarizes the effect that factory farming has on our water: "The [livestock] sector is probably the largest source of water pollution, contributing to eutrophication (dead zones) in coastal areas, degradation of coral reefs, human health problems, emergence of antibiotic resistance, and many others. The major sources of pollution are from animal wastes, antibiotics and hormones, chemicals from tanneries, fertilizers and pesticides used for feedcrops, and sediments from eroded pastures."[212]

LAND

Like our air and water, our land is yet another casualty of the livestock industry. There are two main ways that the livestock industry degrades our land: Through pastures, and through growing feed for the animals.

Pastures

Much of our land degradation is through cattle trampling and defecating on pastureland, and through forests and other natural vegetation getting cut down to make way for new pastures. However, dairy cows are generally confined indoors most (if not all) of the time, and chickens are never in pastures on factory farms. Therefore, if you're not eating meat, you have a very small effect on our land degradation through pasture use.

Growing Feed

However, dairy cows and laying hens do eat billions of pounds of feed, as we've discussed in depth. Growing all this feed not only affects our air and water, it also has a major effect on our land. Specifically, growing feed for the dairy and egg industries causes deforestation, soil erosion, deterioration of soil properties and loss of natural vegetation and biodiversity. Let's discuss each of these...

Deforestation

People cut down forests not only to make way for new pastureland, but also to make way for new fields to grow more animal feed. As we have discussed, cutting down forests has many affects, most notably global warming. When we cut down forests, they are no longer available to help recycle carbon dioxide, and the levels of carbon dioxide in our atmosphere increase, making our planet warmer.

Dairy cows and laying hens eat incredible quantities of feed, and this demand for feed is a major source of global warming. According to the United Nations, "Demand for feedgrains ... has greatly increased the land requirements of livestock production, from a very small area to about 34% of the total arable land today."[213] They estimate up to a 33% increase in cropland between the late 1990's and 2030.[214]

Soil Erosion

Because land is expensive and profit margins are low, there is increased pressure on farmers to grow more crops on the same amount of land. This pressure incentivizes farmers to cut costs by using poor land management techniques. By using heavy machinery, cutting down all natural vegetation and not changing (rotating) their crops each season, they can cause changes in the structure of the soil, landscape morphology, vegetation cover, wind levels, and runoff water, which all lead to soil erosion.

Soil erosion also occurs when the natural vegetation – bushes and trees – is stripped from the land to make room for growing crops. Natural vegetation protects the soil, and their roots bind the soil so it stays in place. When there is no vegetation to protect and bind the soil, the soil gets swept away with the slightest wind. When you drive through cropland where there are no longer any trees or vegetation, you'll notice the frequent dust storms that arise – this is the topsoil being blown off the land. In severe cases, the land can become unsuitable for farming. Perhaps the most extreme case of soil erosion occurred in the 1930's around the Oklahoma panhandle, when farmers stripped the land of all vegetation to make way for wheat fields. Massive dust storms, hundreds of feet high, swept the topsoil off the newly flattened area, sometimes depositing the dust as far away as the White House. The area became unsuitable for living, and many people left the area, often heading to California, as John Steinbeck's *The Grapes of Wrath* describes.

When soil erodes, it can blow off into nearby waterways, causing extreme devastation to the local marine life and ecosystem. It can:

- Increase sedimentation in waterways, resulting in clogged waterways and drainage and irrigation systems.
- Destroy marine habitats, which can become covered in silt and sediments, covering up food sources and nesting sites.
- Disrupt the hydraulic characteristics of waterways.
- Transport nutrients down waterways, accelerating the pollution process.
- Cause eutrophication (dead zones.)[215]

In the U.S., the livestock sector is responsible for approximately 55% of soil erosion, and soil erosion is regarded as one of the most important environmental problems in the U.S. in the last 200 years.[216]

Deterioration of Soil Properties

Cutting down forests to make room to grow feed also affects the integrity of the soil in the area. Soil is packed with nutrients and organic matter that help life to grow. Organic matter in the soil allows nutrients to release and is very important for soil structure and reducing erosion. Gardeners will tell you that it is very hard to grow plants if the soil is not healthy. Because trees add organic matter to the soil (for example, by dropping leaves), deforestation reduces organic matter in the soil, making the soil less fertile.

Ironically, reduced soil fertility makes it harder to grow crops; farmers cut down forests to grow more crops, but the soil then has less fertility and is less productive at growing those crops. South Asia has experienced a loss of productivity from their land that has been directly linked to intensive cropping. Poor land management there has led to the build-up of salinity, waterlogging the soil, declining soil fertility, increased soil toxicity and increased pest populations.

Loss of Natural Vegetation and Biodiversity

In a natural environment, trees and plants help protect the land from the sun and wind. Leaves on the trees provide shade that keeps the temperature down and helps slow the evaporation rate; leaves on the ground help to collect water so it can seep slowly into the ground and be used by the plants. When large areas of trees and plants are completely cut down to grow crops, the leaves are no longer there to protect the land. When it rains on an area that has been cleared of all its trees, the wind and the sun evaporates the water quickly. This makes the land extremely arid and dry.

As the land becomes drier, many species of plants, insects and animals cannot survive. Animals that used the area for food and shelter die off. Plants that needed the natural environment to survive will die off as well. In fact, land-use change has been cited as the leading cause of biodiversity loss.[217] And while many species die out, other less desirable species – like certain pests and weeds – move in. This means that farmers have to spray additional pesticides and herbicides on the new cropland to grow the plants. Of course, they also need to use more water to grow the plants, since the land is so much drier.

The United Nations reports "…deforestation is one of the main causes of loss of unique plant and animal species in the tropical rainforests of Central and South America."[218] They conclude, "The expansion and intensification of crop agriculture is associated with profound land degradation problems."[219]

"When I've heard
all I need to make a decision,
I don't take a vote. I make a decision."
– Ronald Reagan

PART 2

Vegetarian to Vegan: HOW?

To make the change from a vegetarian to a vegan diet, you will need two things: A strong enough reason to do it, and the tools to help you succeed.

Now that you have finished Part 1, you should have a strong enough reason – in fact, many reasons – to give up dairy and egg products forever. But that leaves you with the practical questions about how to do it.

Many people attempting to go vegan give up after one too many challenges, such as eating in restaurants, attending dinner parties, traveling and getting enough protein. To make sure this doesn't happen to you, Part 2 will help you navigate through the challenges that new vegans face, giving you practical strategies to overcome unexpected challenges so that you can go vegan ... and stay vegan.

Let's begin...

"Whether we change our lives
or do nothing, we have responded.
To do nothing is to do something."
– Jonathan Safran Foer

Chapter 6
JUNK VEGAN, HEALTHY VEGAN

Some people go vegan but revert back after feeling like they're weak and not thriving; others may go vegan and stay vegan, but are clearly unhealthy and gaunt. While the goal of this book is to encourage you to go fully vegan, it's essential to your well-being that you do it in a healthy way, so let's begin this "how-to" section on how to be a healthy vegan.

It is possible, although rare, to be unhealthy as a vegan. Eating a diet of french fries, soda, potato chips and candy can be vegan, and while it's preferable to a diet of cheeseburgers and shakes filled not only with saturated fat but also with animal protein, it's clearly still very unhealthy. Even vegan foods can be stuffed full of sugar, salt and fat. Vegan cookies, vegan cakes, French fries and potato chips should be considered a treat, and not eaten every day.

While entire books have been written on how to eat a healthy vegan diet, it's actually very simple and can be summed up in nine bullet points: For the best health benefits – and to feel tons of energy – eat six types of food and limit three:

EAT:	LIMIT:
• Whole beans	• Sugar
• Whole grains	• Salt
• Vegetables	• Fat
• Fruits	
• Nuts	
• Seeds	

FOODS TO EAT

The healthiest foods in the world are whole beans, whole grains, vegetables, fruits, nuts and seeds. They are known, variously, for their high fiber, nutrient and mineral content, their low saturated fat content, and the fact that they do not contain any cholesterol and are generally very low in calories. If you buy almost all of your food out of the produce department and the rice/grains/beans bulk bins, you should be able to stick to a healthy vegan diet quite easily. If you want to buy something that comes in a box, can or bag, check the ingredient list and if anything on the list is not from one of the six bullet points, put it down and make a different choice. Most vegans find that if they focus on what they *can* eat – beans, grains, vegetables, fruits, nuts and seeds – rather than what they can't eat, the vegan diet becomes incredibly simple!

FOODS TO LIMIT

While salt, sugar and some fats (like oil and margarine) are vegan, they are not healthy foods. Additionally, they can be addictive: David Kessler wrote a book called *The End of Overeating*, in which he outlined how the food industry has created addictive combinations of fat, salt and sugar that make us eat and eat and eat. If you've ever sat down with a bag of chips and eaten the whole bag – even though you were not hungry for it – then you've experienced what he's talking about. When you take salt, sugar and fat mostly or completely out of your diet, you will quit having continuous cravings and you will stop overeating. (Note: Fat, when discussed here, is referring to added fat like oil and margarine – not the fat that comes naturally from plant based foods like nuts and seeds.)

> *"I was vegetarian for 35 years and always struggled with weight issues. When I finally made the decision to be vegan I lost 20 lbs. in three months and feel healthier than I ever did as a vegetarian."*
>
> – John Schweri, Nashville, TN

Many westerners have a strong sweet tooth, so giving up sugar will likely be the most psychologically difficult food for many people to give up. However, just 30 days without any sugar or artificial sweeteners will get your tastebuds back to their normal state, and when this happens, you'll be amazed at how good an apple or a carrot will taste. More importantly, you'll be astounded at how your body is finally able to listen to it's own hunger signals, and you quit overeating.

Regarding salt, a good rule of thumb from nutritionist Jeff Novick is to only eat foods that have fewer milligrams of salt than the number of calories per serving. If a food item has 120 calories per serving, it should have <120 mg of salt per serving. Most boxed, bagged and canned food, as well as restaurant food, is full of salt, so as you start following Dr. Novick's advice, you'll find you naturally tend to eat at home more often, and naturally start shopping in the produce and bulk departments more and more.

Fat is the probably the most logistically challenging of the three foods to give up, simply because most prepared vegan foods have oil in them. However, as discussed in Chapter 5, oil can affect your arteries' ability to dilate and contract properly, putting you at risk for heart disease and stroke, so it's important to make this change and limit oil in your diet. There are many alternatives to cooking with oil, such as stir-frying with water or vegetable broth, and using extra water in your baked goods.

If you are struggling to give up dairy and eggs, don't feel like you have to be perfect and give up salt, sugar and fat at the same time. Allowing yourself to eat vegan cheese, soy ice cream and vegan baked goods is a wonderful way to transition from a vegetarian to a vegan diet because these treats help you overcome the psychological fear of giving up your favorite foods. However, subsisting for the long-term on vegan junk food is not a healthy way to live. Use those transition foods to help you move away from eating animal-based foods, and when you're ready, cut back on salt, sugar and fat. If you really stick to it for 30 days, you'll truly be amazed that your cravings are gone, and your old favorite foods will seem unappealing, as they will begin to taste too sugary or too salty.

"The gods created certain kinds
of beings to replenish our bodies; they are
the trees and the plants and the seeds."
– Plato

Chapter 7
PROTEIN AND CALCIUM

One of the most common concerns for aspiring vegans is where they will get their protein and calcium. Because we are taught from a young age that meat = protein and dairy = calcium, it's common for people to assume that a vegan diet is completely devoid of both these important nutrients. Nothing could be further from the truth.

PROTEIN

It's almost always true that if you're getting enough calories, you're getting enough protein. Since the U.S. is certainly packed with people getting plenty of calories, we would not expect to see protein deficiency disease – called kwashiorkor – here very often, and we don't. Even our poor people are usually over-fed. The fact that most people have never heard of kwashiorkor shows how rare it is.

Yet we are bombarded with messages about protein, and it seems that almost everyone is concerned about getting enough

"I have been vegan for 13 months now, and the reason is simply to extend my healthy lifespan. As a 40 year type II diabetic, with good kidney function, healthy heart, healthy eyes, and no other diabetic symptoms, I appreciate the health benefits and the increased energy of being vegan."
- Frank Harris, St. George, UT

of it. Yet you have to ask yourself, where are these messages coming from? It's pretty easy to figure out who's creating all this fuss over getting enough protein, when no one is getting kwashiorkor in developed countries – it's marketing departments in food and supplement companies! They have spent hundreds of millions of dollars getting us to believe that we must supplement our diets with protein bars, protein shakes and protein powders in order to be healthy.

In fact, the truth is that most of us never need to worry about our protein intake at all. Very few people (with the exception of some elite athletes, those with kidney disease and very few others) ever even need to think about their protein intake. If they do need to supplement, it certainly doesn't have to come from animal protein – there are plenty of vegan protein supplements at health food stores.

Physician and best-selling author Joel Fuhrman, MD, suggests we need about 10% of our diet from protein. To see why vegans don't need to be overly concerned with their protein intake, look at the percent of protein in a random sample of fruits, vegetables, nuts and seeds (Table 7.1):

Table 7.1: Protein content in Plant Based Foods

Food	Protein (g) per g of protein per 100 calories	Protein as a % of Calories
Banana	1.22	4.9%
Walnuts	2.33	9.3%
Cashews	3.29	13.2%
Black Beans	6.33	25.3%
Seaweed	6.73	26.9%
Broccoli	8.29	33.2%
Soybeans	8.81	35.2%
Spinach	12.43	49.7%

If you're still not convinced, look at this list of vegan athletes. Athletes are often thought to need high amounts of animal protein in their diet to build strong muscle mass, yet these world-class vegan athletes (Table 7.2) prove that protein does not need to come from animal products.

If you are still concerned about getting enough protein, test it for yourself. Make sure you are eating a well-balanced, healthy vegan diet that includes beans, nuts and seeds, and see if you feel weak or lack strength after a couple of months. In the unlikely case that you do, you can always add a vegan protein supplement to your diet.

Table 7.2: Vegan Athletes

Vegan Athlete	Sport	Claim to Fame
Martina Navratilova	Tennis	Most Grand Slam Wins in History
Carl Lewis	Track & Field	10 Olympic Medals and 10 World Records in Track and Field
Scott Jurek	Ultra-Marathon Runner	World Record Holding Ultra-Marathoner
John Sally	Basketball	Four-time NBA Champion
Billy Simmons	Body Building	2009 Mr. Natural Universe
Arian Foster	Football	2010 NFL Rushing Leader
Serena Williams	Tennis	Multiple Grand Slam Champion and Olympic Gold Medal Winner
Patrik Baboumian	Powerlifting	World Record Powerlifting Champion
Rich Roll	Ultra-Triathlete	Completed 5 Ironman Triathlons in 7 Days.

CALCIUM

Like protein, we are taught to believe that we must be diligent about getting enough calcium – especially women, who have a higher risk for osteoporosis later in life. However, as we discussed in Chapter 5, it is a fallacy that dairy products help bone health. At best they don't affect it, and at worst, they are highly detrimental to bone health.

It is true that calcium is important for building and maintaining strong bones, and it's also important for strong teeth, blood clotting, transmitting nerve impulses and regulating the heart's rhythm, among other things. 99% of calcium in the human body is stored in the bones and teeth.[220] So we do need to get enough calcium, but we don't need to get it from dairy products. Where does one find a healthy source of calcium in a vegan diet? All over the place! Lots of fruits and vegetables have calcium in them, but dark leafy greens – the powerhouses of the nutritional world – supply the highest amounts, along with many beans and legumes. Table 7.3 shows some common fruits, vegetables, nuts and seeds and their calcium content.

Table 7.3: Calcium content in Plant Based Foods

Food	Calcium (mg) per 100g of food
Banana	5 mg
Cashews	37 mg
Broccoli	47 mg
Walnuts	98 mg
Spinach	99 mg
Black Beans	123 mg
Seaweed – Kelp	168 mg
Soybeans	277 mg

Despite what the men's and women's magazines would have you believe, you shouldn't need to obsess about your protein or calcium intake every day. Eating a variety of fruits, vegetables, beans, grains, nuts and seeds every day should give most people the protein and calcium that their bodies need. If you are still concerned, have your doctor follow your health, especially in your first year or two as a vegan.

> *"Going from vegetarian to vegan opened my body, mind, and soul to living with respect and compassion for all the inhabitants of our planet."*
> – Lorri Houston, Los Angeles, CA

"I do not regard flesh-food as necessary for us at any stage and under any clime in which it is possible for human beings ordinarily to live. I hold flesh-food to be unsuited to our species."
– Mahatma Ghandi

Chapter 8

VITAMIN B$_{12}$

Vitamin B$_{12}$ (also known as cobalamin) is the only supplement that most doctors universally recommend for vegans. Vitamin B$_{12}$ is important for normal functioning of the nerves and brain, the formation of blood, the metabolism of cells, as well as fatty acid synthesis and energy production. It is not readily found in the vegan diet.

When people first hear that an important vitamin like B$_{12}$ is not readily found in a vegan diet, they often assume that the vegan diet must not be the perfect diet for humans after all. Yet when people learn *why* the vegan diet generally doesn't contain vitamin B$_{12}$, they usually change their minds...

Vitamin B$_{12}$ comes from bacteria. Thousands of years ago, humans didn't wash their vegetables before eating them. Therefore, they ended up eating a lot of the dirt that was on the vegetables, and that dirt had beneficial bacteria in it, containing vitamin B$_{12}$.

Today, we obviously wash our vegetables carefully: We have pre-bagged spinach that is "triple-washed," we have little potato scrubbers next to our sinks to scrub dirt off our potatoes, and we can even buy special "soap"

"I always said, 'I will never go vegan. I simply cannot do without cheese.' Well, never say never! One day, I just decided to do it. I went through a period where I was "detoxing" from dairy; I felt mildly sick, feverish and had a runny nose all the time. It was all that mucus leaving my body! Once it all got out, my tastes totally changed, my triglycerides went from 180 to below 80, and I feel GREAT!!!!!"

- Karen Beth Martin, Corinth, MS

to wash our produce! So the vegetables we find in today's supermarkets do not have dirt on them, and therefore do not have the vitamin B_{12} that we need for our health.

"When I first went vegetarian, I was shocked that people told me it wasn't enough! You have got to be kidding, I thought. This was a huge step I'd taken! But when I finally gave up dairy, after learning about the cruel lives of dairy cows and their calves, I was even more shocked. I lost 18 pounds, my skin cleared up, my nails stopped breaking and my energy levels went sky high. I ran a marathon the year I gave up dairy, having never run more than 6 miles before that."

– Patti Breitman, Fairfax, CA

Yet when a cow eats grass, for example, it pulls the grass up from the ground and there is still dirt left on the roots of that grass; the cow then gets Vitamin B_{12} by eating that dirt. When humans eat the cow's meat or dairy products, they get vitamin B_{12}. This is why vitamin B_{12} is found in meat and vegetarian-based diets, but not in a vegan diet.

Our bodies only need trace amounts of vitamin B_{12} to be healthy. It takes months or years to store up vitamin B_{12} levels in our body, and it also takes months or years to deplete those levels. However, Vitamin B_{12} levels are something to take very seriously: Vitamin B_{12} deficiency has been linked with serious and irreversible nerve and brain damage, fatigue, depression, memory loss, mania and psychosis among other things. On the flip side, high levels of vitamin B_{12} may be protective against Alzheimer's Disease.[221] Since the damage from low B_{12} is often irreversible, it's definitely not worth taking a chance – take your vitamin B_{12} supplements.

Many vegans prefer not to take supplements and instead opt for the few vegan sources of B_{12} that are available: fortified foods like cereals, soy products, tempeh, spirulina and nutritional yeast. Fortified foods are similar to taking a supplement – the vitamin B$_{12}$ has been added to a food that otherwise doesn't naturally contain it, and this is fine. However, the UK Vegan Society says that the vitamin B$_{12}$ from "natural" vegan sources (like unfortified nutritional yeast and spirulina) is not likely to be available to humans because vitamin B$_{12}$ analogues can compete with the vitamin B$_{12}$ and inhibit metabolism.[222,223] So again, it's important to supplement with a vitamin B$_{12}$ tablet to be on the safe side.

When shopping for vitamin B$_{12}$ tablets, make sure that you read the ingredient list – many B$_{12}$ supplements have dairy products in them! Your local health food store should be able to help you find a vegan source of vitamin B$_{12}$.

"There is nothing so powerful
as an idea whose time has come."
– Victor Hugo

Chapter 9

DINING AT RESTAURANTS

Many vegetarians think that when they go vegan their social life will end and all their weekend dinners out will come to a halt. Nothing could be further from the truth! There are amazing vegan restaurants popping up all over the place, and many of them are offering very healthy options that are low in salt, sugar and fat. Even non-vegan restaurants are becoming vegan-savvy, offering delicious dinners that will make your dining companions want what you ordered!

In case you end up in a restaurant that doesn't have vegan entrees on the menu, here are some tips from *Vegan in 30 Days* on how to make sure you don't get stuck with white rice and steamed carrots for dinner:

> *"I became a vegetarian when I was 12, and went vegan over 4 years ago when I was 36. Even as a vegetarian, I'd suffered from debilitating migraines that wiped me out for two days each month. The day I went vegan the migraines stopped and I've never had one since."*
>
> – Susan Bennett, Stamford, UK

1. **Call ahead.** Ask the hostess to tell the chef that you are vegan, and tell them when you'll be dining there. They will appreciate the heads-up, and you will probably get a better meal, since the chef will have had time to think about it. Don't forget to tell them specifically what vegans don't eat, just in case they think vegans are the same as vegetarians, and also remember to tell them what a vegan *does* eat, so they think

beyond just veggies and rice. If you are committed to eating a really healthy vegan diet and don't want to end up with white pasta or oily vegetables for example, calling ahead is highly recommended so the chef has time to think of something to suit your needs.

2. **Scan the menu for vegan items.** Pasta primavera, veggie sushi or stir-fry noodles with veggies and tofu are all popular options. Salads with a vinaigrette dressing are always a good stand-by, and can be found at almost any restaurant. If you've never had pizza without cheese, extra red sauce and extra veggies, you'll be amazed at what you were missing all these years! If you're worried you just couldn't survive pizza without cheese, try bringing a bag of Daiya vegan cheese to your favorite pizzeria, and asking them to use it on your pizza. This will give you the pizza you want, and also allow the chef to try a new product that the restaurant may want to add as an option on their menu!

3. **Tell them what you want – even if it's nowhere on the menu.** If fruit is not on the menu for dessert, ask for it anyway – chances are you'll get it. If pasta primavera is nowhere to be found on the menu, ask for it anyway – chances are you'll get it. You get the idea!

4. **Look for easy substitutions.** For example, Chinese Chicken Salad without the chicken, or a vegetarian burrito without the sour cream and cheese. You'll be surprised at what tastes great, even without the dairy products you thought you could never give up.

5. **Look for options from non-vegan items that you can combine to make vegan.** For example, if the menu has Spaghetti Bolognese, and Chicken with Vegetables, ask for Spaghetti with Vegetables. You can also look at all the different side dishes that come with the main entrees, and ask the waiter

to make you a full meal of vegan side dishes.

6. **Ask the chef to get creative and make whatever he or she wants.** This may end up being one of your favorite options because you'll often get the most delicious dinners if you just let the chef get creative. This is almost a guaranteed winner in better restaurants.

"I was a vegetarian for 20 years when I was diagnosed with Systemic Lupus. It was a wake-up call! I went on a totally raw, vegan diet and within 90 days, my blood transformed and the Lupus seemed to vanish! My café, the Leafy Greens Café, is the reflection of my conviction towards better health and a better world. I know that I am doing what's best now – for myself, for the animals and for the planet."
- Denise Rispoli Becknell, St Petersburg FL

If you are traveling, the best way to avoid ending up at a restaurant without good vegan options is to get on the internet and search for vegan restaurants in the cities you will be visiting. A simple search like "vegan restaurants in Chicago" will return multiple options, and take you directly to websites that specialize in following vegan restaurants, like HappyCow. net. You will find vegan restaurants all over the world, and will likely make great memories and friends when you go!

"Nothing of any real positive social value
has ever been achieved from the top down;
it's always been achieved from the bottom up."
– Howard Zinn

Chapter 10

ENTERTAINING

Many people like to entertain at home or be a guest at other people's homes. In order to make it easy for everyone, here are some tips that will help, whether you are hosting or are a guest.

BEING A VEGAN HOST

When hosting a dinner or party, you'll need to think ahead about what type of food you will serve, and whether you'll keep a strict vegan household. If you'll allow meat and dairy in your house, make a great meal or hors d'ouvres that have both non-vegan and vegan options. Make sure you include several vegan dishes, as people will be curious about your diet and will want to try vegan food. Be sure to make your best recipes to show them that vegan food can be really delicious! You can guarantee that most people will be skeptical; this is your chance to abolish their skepticism.

However, allowing meat and dairy products in your house may go against your values, especially after everything you've learned in Part 1. If you would rather that your house be 100% vegetarian or 100% vegan, have the courage to set that rule, and make sure your guests know this ahead of time. Obviously this is crucial if you are

> *"For ethical reasons I went vegetarian in 1950, but without any knowledge of nutrition. When I came out of medical school in 1964 I still didn't know much nutrition but it had finally sunk in that to get milk you have to keep the cow pregnant, so I went vegan. Then strangely, all my chronic allergies and constant colds went away. So what I thought was a big sacrifice turned out to be a huge present to myself."*
> – Bill Harris, M.D.

having a potluck, but even if you're doing all the cooking, people may bring milk chocolates, smoked salmon or other gifts of food for you as the hostess, and you wouldn't want to embarrass them if they found out that you keep a vegan or vegetarian house.

> *"After many months of being bedridden with arthritis, going from vegetarian to vegan gave me back the ability to walk. The difference has been nothing short of miraculous. Thirteen years later, I'm still walking."*
>
> - Cathy Bryant, Manchester, UK

Early on it may seem uncomfortable not to allow meat, dairy and eggs in your house, but it won't take long before your friends and family will get used to your new lifestyle. If people push back, stand your ground; you will feel better for sticking to your values and not capitulating to peer pressure. You'll be surprised at how many people will tell you how much they respect your decision!

BEING A VEGAN GUEST

It can be awkward for people when they first invite you over for dinner after you've gone vegan – they may not know what to make, they may be worried that you won't like what they make, and they may have an underlying terror that they don't really understand your new diet and that they'll inadvertently feed you something non-vegan. All of this is understandable.

In an effort to make it easy for your host/hostess and less awkward for everyone, here are some tips that you'll both appreciate:

1. If the hostess has not acknowledged that you are vegan, and you think she either may not know or may have forgotten, make sure to bring it up when you RSVP. Then…

2. Offer to bring your own dish. In fact, you can specifically say that since she will have a lot of other cooking to do, you would be happy to bring your own dish, with enough for everyone

for share. If she agrees to let you bring your own dish, make something really delicious that can be a complete meal for you, and also appropriate for everyone else as a side dish, such as a vegan risotto or paella. If you bring a fabulous dish people will be more open to learning about the vegan diet – you've just shown them that vegan food is really good!

> *"The transition to a vegan diet isn't difficult. In fact it cuts out all the compromise that was previously part of my decision process. It's guilt-free."*
> – Anthony Phelps, Manchester, UK

3. However, if the hostess is really relishing the challenge of making a true vegan meal and tells you not to bring your own dish, then oblige and tell her what vegans can and cannot eat. Suggest a few websites where she might find recipes, let her have fun, and enjoy the treat!

"Be who you are and say what you feel,
because those who mind don't matter,
and those who matter don't mind."
– Dr. Seuss

Chapter 11
TRAVELING

A relatively common concern for vegetarians who are considering the vegan diet is their travel schedule. Many people say, "I'd love to be vegan, but I travel too much and it's too hard." In fact, traveling as a vegan can be surprisingly easy, even in the most unlikely places. Whether you travel for work or leisure, vegan food is everywhere – you just have to uncover it!

TRAVELING FOR WORK

Traveling for work can require special attention as you navigate around airports and train stations, and dine with important clients and colleagues. Here are some ideas to help you manage:

- Dining out. When eating at restaurants for work, refer to Chapter 10 for suggestions on dining out at restaurants: learn to scan the menu for vegan options and substitutes, ask for exceptions, or ask the chef to make you something that is not on the menu.

- Plan ahead. If you have an important dinner planned where you want business – not your diet – to be the focus of attention, you'll want to plan ahead. Always try to make a reservation so you know where you'll be dining, and make sure to investigate the restaurant's menu online or call ahead to make sure that you'll get a vegan dinner without a lengthy discussion with the waiter in front of your clients. You can even arrive early and finalize your order with your waiter so you won't have to bring your diet up at dinner at all.

- Eating on your own. When you don't have to dine in "regular" restaurants with colleagues or clients, it can be a great time to try out vegan restaurants. If you travel a lot, you'll get to try gourmet vegan options all around the country! You can also consider bringing your own food, or eating at a natural foods deli or store. Eating in a natural food store's deli is a great option, especially if you are committed to eating a healthy diet, and are avoiding salt, sugar and oil. Many vegan businesspeople also remember to stop at a natural foods deli before boarding a train or plane, so they will have a great meal while they travel.

TRAVELING FOR PLEASURE

When traveling for pleasure, many of the same guidelines for business travel can apply, and vice versa. Here are some added tips to assist you:

- Research online. When going to a new city, Google "Vegan restaurants in [name of city] for a list of vegan, vegetarian, and veg-friendly establishments.

- Seek out ethnic restaurants. Many ethnic restaurants naturally have a lot of vegetarian options due to cultural and religious preferences around the world. Great options are Indian (request no dairy), Thai (request no fish or shrimp sauce) Japanese and Chinese (request no egg.)

- Call ahead. If you'll be on a tour, call your tour guides well ahead of time about your diet, and follow up two or three times before the trip to make sure they have remembered. One safari company (The Africa Adventure Company) famously called ahead to their camps before a vegan traveler was scheduled to arrive, and one camp ordered soymilk from France and had it shipped into the Zimbabwe bush, whereupon the cook made a vegan casserole and a cake with vegan frosting, among many other vegan delights!

- Don't be too picky. Be easygoing about your diet, and let your hosts know that you will be happy with simple fare like fruit, toast, salad and rice and beans, for example. They will likely be very appreciative and feel much less stress.

- Pack your own food. Bring as much food as you can to get you through your trip, especially dense foods like nuts that can tide you over for a few hours if you're really hungry. Here's a good tip for U.S. travelers: a grocery bag of food does not count toward your carry on bag limit in the U.S., so you can board a long flight with an entire bag filled with veggies, hummus, sandwiches and other items you love!

> *"I've been eating a vegan diet for nearly 10 years (after being vegetarian for 20 years). I've never felt better – I've maintained the same weight (without dieting) and I've had absolutely no eczema. I have heaps of energy and am never sick – being vegan definitely benefits my health!"*
>
> – Lisa Drummy, Hants, UK

- Traveling off the beaten path. If you're going to a developing country, you will likely have more – not less – vegan options, as many poorer countries cannot afford to eat meat and dairy products regularly, so their national dishes are often naturally vegan. Rice and Beans, Baba Ganoush, Hummus, Nasi Goreng and Faal are examples.

Whether you are traveling for work or pleasure, it may seem overwhelming at first to find vegan options, but you will soon learn where they are. Just like a person who is following a fat-free diet, a low-salt diet or any other specific diet, eating vegan on the road simply requires a little dedication up front to finding options. Once you have done it a few times it gets easier, and eventually, traveling as a vegan will become second-nature to you.

"The problem with following the herd
is stepping in what it leaves behind."
– Keith Cunningham

Chapter 12
DAIRY, EGG AND HONEY SUBSTITUTES

Out of all the reasons people give for not being able to go vegan, the most common is that they don't believe they can ever live without their favorite dairy products, especially cheese. It can definitely seem daunting after giving up all meat, poultry and fish, to also give up dairy, eggs and honey. However, as with most things, we tend to worry greatly about things that never end up being half the problem we thought they would be. Even if you do struggle at first, once you've been vegan for a month or two you will have new favorite foods, new recipes to draw from and will have learned how to cook your old favorites using vegan alternatives. At this point, being vegan will be fairly effortless.

Here are some quick substitutes to get you started, and Chef Mark Reinfeld has offered even more suggestions in the recipe section. The more you experiment and check out new recipes and vegan websites online, the quicker you will acclimate to your new substitute products and know how and when to use them

"Since going from vegetarian to vegan, I have more energy and need less sleep. I also recover from workouts faster, and have more stamina on the ice."
– Mike Zigomanis, Toronto Maple Leafs, Toronto, Canada

DAIRY SUBSTITUTES
The vegan diet is becoming so popular that many stores carry a host of vegan options. Soy milk, rice milk, tofu and other vegan alternatives are becoming commonplace.

Milk

When it comes to a milk substitution, you may need to experiment with a few types and brands. Milk alternatives are one area where the taste varies widely. Therefore, if you try a brand of soymilk and don't like it, try another brand or try almond milk or rice milk instead, for example. It's fairly common for vegans to report trying two or three different brands of soymilk to find the one they like best. The different types of milk substitutes can also be used in baking, or you may choose to just use water.

- Soymilk
- Almond Milk
- Rice Milk
- Hemp Milk
- Coconut Milk
- Oat Milk
- Water

Butter

The vegan options for butter are so good that most people never notice the difference. There are several brands of vegan "butter" that can be used in cooking, baking or straight on food, and it's not likely that you will be able to taste the difference. Here are some alternatives for using butter, but – like butter – they are not necessarily healthy:

- Vegan Butter Spread (Earth Balance is extremely popular)
- Margarine
- Oil
- Nut Butters (Peanut Butter, Almond Butter, etc)

Cheese

Out of all the things that vegetarians fear giving up, cheese is probably the biggest. Not long ago, there were few options for vegan cheese alternatives that actually were edible, but fortunately, that has changed.

When cooking, nutritional yeast gives a very cheesy flavor, and is usually a main ingredient in dishes like vegan macaroni and cheese and vegan casseroles. If you want a ready-to-eat product for a grilled cheese sandwich, for example, there are now cheese substitutes that will fool any cheese lover! Daiya brand cheese (cheddar and Havarti are outstanding) has revolutionized vegan eating. You can also make your own nut cheeses right at home, which will surprise you with their likeness to real cheese. Beware that most soy cheeses are not vegan – they contain casein or whey, which are animal proteins. Check out the internet and vegan cookbooks for some amazing recipes for your favorite cheeses. Here are a few cheese substitutes for your current recipes:

- Vegan Cheese Products
- Nut cheese (like Cashew Cheese)
- Nutritional Yeast

Other Dairy Products

There are plenty of great alternatives in your natural foods store for most of your favorite dairy products. Try out different brands and ask the workers at the store for the most popular brands.

- Vegan Yogurt (including Greek yogurt)
- Vegan Mayonnaise
- Vegan Sour Cream
- Vegan Cream Cheese
- Vegan Ice Cream

EGG SUBSTITUTES

While there are really no vegan substitutes for a fried or hard-boiled egg, eggs can be substituted in most recipes. Crumbled tofu can make a fantastic alternative to scrambled eggs (check out the recipe section in Part 3!) If you enjoy baking, there are a multitude of options for alternative binding agents, as you'll find listed below. Don't be afraid to experiment – some boxes of bake mix call for an egg and milk, for example, but if you leave them both out altogether and add some water instead for moisture, you'll still get a very good result!

Egg Substitutes in Baking:

- Egg Substitute Products (such as EnerG Egg Replacer)
- Tofu
- Applesauce
- Banana
- Flour + Water
- Flaxmeal
- Arrowroot Powder
- Agar Powder

HONEY SUBSTITUTES

Honey is used fairly frequently as a sweetener. It is often found in cereal, bread, baked goods, glazes, marinades and sauces, among other places. Syrups are a great substitute for honey, whether you like to drizzle honey directly onto your food, or use it in baking or cooking.

If you are buying sweetened foods at the store, be careful to read labels carefully, especially on cereal boxes, in the bread aisle and the bakery department. Look for items marked "vegan" and you can rest assured they won't have honey. However, be careful to avoid this trap: Some products proclaim "Dairy and Egg Free!" If it's obviously not a meat product, it is easy to assume this product must be vegan. However, if it doesn't specifically say it's vegan, it is likely that there is honey in the ingredient list.

Below are some alternatives to honey that you can use on your food and in your baked goods:

- Agave Syrup
- Maple Syrup

- Golden Syrup
- Date Syrup
- Sugar
- Date Sugar

With very few exceptions, anything you can eat as a vegetarian, you can eat as a vegan. Most importantly, the vegan options are usually just as delicious as the vegetarian ones! This can be hard to believe until you've tried it, so if you're skeptical, you can easily convince yourself that this is true in just one meal: Go to a gourmet vegan restaurant with a couple of other people and order all the "cheesy" foods, baked foods and ice creams. In a really gourmet vegan restaurant, you should *never* notice the difference between vegan and vegetarian foods. The macaroni and "cheese" at *Sublime* in Fort Lauderdale, the "calamari" (oyster mushrooms) with "aoli" sauce at *Millennium* in San Francisco, the "cheese" platter at *Madeline's* in the Los Angeles area and the cookies, cakes and ice creams at all these restaurants will convince you that you truly *won't* have to live without! If you don't live near a restaurant like these, don't fret! Part 3 is packed with recipes from award winning chef Mark Reinfeld that will allow you to make this point right in your own home. The vegan diet has come a long way, and it's never been easier – or tastier – to be a vegan.

> *"My doctor told me my total cholesterol was 191 which he said was borderline high. I had just started eating a vegetarian diet (which included eggs and dairy) and on a follow up check I was still in the 180's. He said that since my family has a history of high cholesterol, I would always be battling with it. I switched to a vegan diet and after 6 months my cholesterol had gone down to 150. My last check was 138."*
>
> – Greg Rohrbach RN, BSN, San Francisco, CA

"Never doubt that a small group of thoughtful, committed citizens can change the world; indeed, it's the only thing that ever has."
– Margaret Mead

CONCLUSION

In the time of Copernicus, the majority of people believed the sun revolved around the Earth, and they were wrong. In the time of Galileo, the majority of people believed the Earth was flat, and they were wrong. In recent years, the majority of people believed smoking was harmless and ulcers were caused by stress, and they, too, were wrong.

There are countless examples in both past and recent history when the majority of people believed very strongly in certain "facts," only to discover later that they had been dead wrong. Perhaps that is why Mark Twain once said, "When you find yourself on the side of the majority, it's time to pause and reflect."

I believe that the majority of people today believe that "milk does a body good." I think the majority of people today believe that we need to eat meat (or eggs) to get enough protein, and we need to eat dairy to get enough calcium. I think the majority of people today believe that factory farms can't be too inhumane because the government would certainly step in and stop companies from treating animals cruelly. I think the majority of people today believe that paying higher prices for cage-free, free-range and organic dairy and egg products ensure that the animals were raised humanely. I think the majority of people today don't believe that the animal agriculture industry has a large effect on our environment. In all these cases and more, I believe the majority of people today are wrong.

I hope you can now see that, despite what companies want you to believe about the dairy and egg products they are selling, the truth is that these products are terrible for your health, terrible for our environment, and in almost all cases, are unconscionably cruel to animals.

We have seen evidence that almost all dairy and egg products come from cows and hens in factory farming conditions, and that these conditions are almost universally inhumane. Dairy cows are kept crammed into small pens on hard floors, susceptible to diseases and viruses from other cows living in close proximity. They live a life of constant pregnancy and birth, and the tiny bit of joy they must feel when they see their babies for the first time is quickly aborted, as the babies are whisked out of the birthing pen just 2 hours after birth. The incredible toll on the cows' bodies of being constantly pregnant, lactating and living in unnatural conditions can result in a very common and painful infection of the udder called mastitis. It can also lead to low calcium levels that develop into milk fever, an infection of the uterus called endometritis, and many foot and leg problems that can cause them to go lame. The crowding in dairy factory farms ensures that viruses and bacteria can spread quickly from cow to cow. Cows on a factory farm – but not in nature – are very susceptible to getting bovine immunodeficiency virus, bovine leukemia virus, and paratuberculosis (Johne's disease).

Like dairy cows, egg laying hens are also kept packed together – whether they are in battery cages or not – usually never feeling the sunlight on their backs, the wind in their feathers, or having enough room to spread their wings. Their conditions make it impossible for them to establish a pecking order amongst their flock, which can lead to extreme psychological frustration. This frustration leads them to attack each other, pecking at each other's feathers, cloaca, and often cannibalizing each other. The psychological stress of being crowded together also causes behaviors unseen in nature, like the repetitive movements of stereoptypies, self-mutilation through feather plucking, and sham dustbathing.

Battery cages are stacked on top of one another, allowing urine and feces to fall on all the birds that are not in the top row. This configuration of cages, added to the crowding of so many animals under one roof, leads to a host of medical problems: High rates of disease and infection, feet that get melded to the wire floors, and cage layer osteoporosis. In an attempt to reduce the incidence of all of these issues, farmers slice off the hens' beaks to keep them from mutilating each other, dim the lights so they cannot see each other's sores and cannibalize each other, and pump them full of antibiotics.

To increase their productivity, layer hens are often forced to molt all of their feathers at once; this forced molt happens by depriving the birds of food and water for up to 14 days. Sadly, the tiny males chicks born at the hatcheries are ground up alive or thrown into dumpsters to suffocate because they are not useful as meat and cannot lay eggs.

In the end, both dairy cows and egg laying hens go to the exact same slaughterhouses as cows and chickens raised for their meat. They are slaughtered – often alive – at the end of all this horror.

In addition to animal welfare issues, we saw evidence of the health effects that dairy and egg products have on humans. Dairy and eggs have been linked over and over in the medical literature with:

- cancer, including breast, ovarian, uterine, prostate, liver and other cancers.

- heart disease

- osteoporosis

- multiple sclerosis

- type I and type II diabetes

- lactose intolerance

- and many other medical conditions…

While it's bad enough that these foods are causing so much death and disease, it's arguably much worse that they are advertised as some of the healthiest foods on the planet. Nothing could be further from the truth, as the list above demonstrates.

Finally, we discussed the environment, and the impact that dairy and egg farms have on our air, water and soil. The dairy and egg industries have been directly associated with global warming; millions of acres of trees that recycle carbon dioxide are getting cut down to make way to grow food for dairy cows and egg laying hens. Global warming is causing entire island nations and coastal towns to flood, polar bears to die off, more frequent and severe weather disasters and entire ecosystems to die off.

Manure from billions of dairy cows and laying hens harm the air quality in local towns, and people suffer from high rates of asthma and respiratory illness. Manure spills are very common, and get into nearby ground water wells and waterways, causing illness and death of both humans and marine life.

Growing feed for billions of animals uses up so much water around the world that environmentalists warn that many aquifers will dry up in the coming decades. The feed crops are also sprayed with fertilizer, which gets into our waterways and kills of billions of fish, creating massive "dead zones" around the world where fish and marine life can no longer survive. Poor land management techniques from the crop farmers creates soil erosion, deterioration of the soil's properties, and a loss of biodiversity in our animal, insect and plant life.

While it can be hard to look at a little bit of cheese on your burrito or a splash of creamer in your coffee and imagine that it can do much harm, my sincere hope is that you will now see a new reality. I hope that when you see a carton of eggs in the grocery store – even "organic" and "free-range" eggs – you will now remember the hens who suffered greatly to provide those eggs. I hope that when you pass an ice cream or frozen yogurt store, you will now remember the cows who agonized to provide those treats. I hope that when you see a carton of milk – even fat-free milk – sitting on a grocery shelf, you will now remember the incredible damage that dairy and egg products are doing to your health and the health of your loved ones. I hope that when you see a block of cheese in the deli case, you will now remember the environmental destruction that occurred to put that cheese on the grocery store shelf.

The good news is that **once we know better, we can do better**. While we have talked about how terrible dairy and egg products are for the animals, our health and our environment, we have also talked about how you can easily quit your dairy and egg habits and still eat delicious food, even when you're traveling, eating in restaraunts or entertaining. There are countless vegan options springing up in grocery stores, delis and restaurants all over the world.

With just a couple of months dedicated to uncovering new products, learning new recipes and making new habits, you will

spend the rest of your life knowing that you are saving lives, avoiding cruelty, helping our planet and enjoying optimum health.

I am honored that you have taken the time to read this book, and so impressed that you care enough to change. I hope our paths cross, and you will tell me your story.

With Love and Ahimsa,
Sarah

"We must become the change
we seek in the world."
– Mahatma Ghandi

PART 3

Vegetarian to Vegan: RECIPES

by Chef Mark Reinfeld

RECIPE CONTENTS

ENTREES

DESSERTS

♥ = Heart Healthy

Introduction to Veganizing Vegetarian Recipes

by *Chef Mark Reinfeld*

I am very happy that Sarah asked me to contribute recipes to Vegetarian to Vegan. I feel that moving from a vegetarian to a vegan diet is an extremely important topic to address, now that the veg revolution is upon us and more people are becoming interested in including healthier plant based foods into their lifestyle.

I feel that those of us who became vegetarian because of our love of animals, our desire to conserve the Earth's resources, and or our desire for optimal health, need to continually examine how our food choices support these intentions. It is crystal clear to me that making a shift to a completely plant based diet is the next logical step in this journey towards a more compassionate and sustainable way of living.

Fortunately for everyone, going vegan is easier than ever. As a vegan chef for the past twenty years, it has been one of my highest priorities to demonstrate that a shift towards plant-based cuisine can be a world-class, gourmet culinary adventure.

Many vegetarian items such as dairy and eggs can easily be substituted with vegan alternatives. Here are a few simple substitutions:

- **Milk** – plant based milks including almond, hemp, rice, soy, oat, or coconut. For a homemade nut or seed milk recipe, please see page 187.

- **Butter** – Earth Balance is my favorite commercially available brand

- **Buttermilk** – Combine 1 cup of vegan milk plus 1 tablespoon of freshly squeezed lemon juice, and allow to stand for 10 minutes before using in a recipe

- **Eggs** – Try using 1 tablespoon of ground flax seeds mixed with 3 tablespoons of water for each egg a recipe calls for. Mashed bananas, apple sauce, and silken tofu can also be used to replace eggs in baking, as can Ener-G Egg Replacer.

- **Mayonnaise** – Vegenaise is my favorite commercially available brand, or you can experiment with a home made version on page 191.

For aspiring vegans, I often encourage people to experiment with including what I like to call 'transitional foods' or analogue products. These are foods such as vegan mayonnaise, vegan butter, vegan cheese, vegan ice cream, faux meat products, etc. that are not necessarily healthy, but provide a similar taste and texture to the animal product they aim to replace.

An important aspect in making long lasting changes to your diet is to never feel deprived along the way. The world of vegan analogue products has undergone a radical and positive transformation over the last twenty years. These foods can help satisfy cravings when they do arise and allow you to feel satiated. Over time, I encourage people to strive for a more wholesome, less processed menu and only use these transitional products minimally or in moderation, as Sarah has also addressed.

I would also like to introduce the concept of a template recipe. It's a way of breaking a recipe down into its component parts. You can create countless variations by altering the different components of the dish. It is the technique that I emphasize in the 10-day Vegan Fusion Culinary Immersions I have been offering around the country. The Mediterranean Pistachio Crusted Tofu with Saffron Quinoa Pilaf (see page 225) is a perfect example of a template recipe where, by altering any of the components, you can create a new dish:

- **Tofu component:** The tofu can be replaced with tempeh, Portobello mushrooms, eggplant, or zucchini steaks.

- **Marinade component:** Alter the marinade by adding additional ingredients such as maple syrup, balsamic vinegar, brown rice vinegar, mirin, curry paste, or your favorite fresh herbs.

- **Tahini spread component:** Replace the tahini with almond butter, peanut butter, or another nut butter. Replace the lemon with lime juice. Add additional ingredients such as minced garlic, ginger, or various ethnic spices.

- **Crust component:** The pistachio nuts can be replaced with any nut or seed such as macadamias, walnuts, pecans, hazelnuts, sunflower seeds, pumpkin seeds, or sesame seeds. These can be raw or roasted. You can replace the herbs with your favorites such as cilantro, basil, or dill. You can also create various ethnic crusts by adding spices from various cuisines (Mexican: chile powder, cumin, oregano; Italian: basil, parsley, oregano, rosemary, thyme; Indian: curry powder, cumin powder, and ground coriander).

- **Pilaf component:** Replace the quinoa with another grain, including millet, any variety of rice, or even brown rice pasta. Add herbs of your choice to the pilaf.

- **Mediterranean Vegetable component:** These vegetables can be replaced with your favorites, either raw, steamed, roasted, sautéed, or grilled.

With that said, I selected these recipes because I feel they represent vegan versions of the types of dishes that vegetarians currently enjoy and where many variations are possible. They are from several sources including my books: *Vegan Fusion World Cuisine, The Complete Idiot's Guide to Eating Raw, The 30 Minute Vegan, The 30 Minute Vegan's Taste of the East,* and *The 30 Minute Vegan's Taste of Europe.* Give them a try and you will find that you can have an incredible array of meals without the use of animal products. Use these recipes as a starting point to develop your own creativity in the kitchen. Above all – have fun with them!

To your health,
Mark Reinfeld

↺ BREAKFAST ↻

♥ Tofu Scrambles
Simple Tofu Scramble

Eggs are so 1980's. This scramble is one of our favorite recipes for introducing folks to tofu. Be sure to use the extra firm tofu and watch as the turmeric creates a vibrant yellow in the dish. So many variations are possible as you can add an ethnic flare to your scrambles as the following recipes demonstrate.

Courtesy of *The 30 Minute Vegan*
Serves 2 to 4

1½ tablespoons safflower oil
1 cup yellow onion, chopped small
4 medium garlic cloves, pressed or minced
14 ounces extra firm tofu, crumbled large
¾ teaspoon turmeric powder
¾ teaspoon paprika
3 tablespoons nutritional yeast
1 ½ teaspoons wheat-free tamari or other soy sauce, or to taste
Sea salt and black pepper to taste

1. Place the oil in a large sauté pan over medium-high heat.
2. Add the onion and garlic and cook until the onions are soft, approximately 3 minutes, stirring frequently.
3. Add the tofu. Cook for 5 minutes, stirring frequently.
4. Add the remaining ingredients and enjoy.

Tofu Scramble Italiano

Courtesy of *The 30 Minute Vegan*
Serves 6

To the simple Tofu Scramble, add the following:

4 large mushrooms, sliced
1 medium tomato, chopped
1 small bunch spinach, rinsed and drained (about 3 cups)
1 ½ tablespoons minced basil
1 teaspoon oregano

Follow the Simple Tofu Scramble recipe. Add the mushrooms in with the onions and garlic. Add the remaining ingredients after cooking the tofu for 5 minutes.

South West Tofu Scramble

Courtesy of *The 30 Minute Vegan*
Serves 4

To the simple Tofu Scramble, add the following:

1 small red bell pepper, chopped small
1 medium jalapeño or other chile pepper, seeded and minced
2 tablespoons minced cilantro
1 ½ teaspoons chile powder, try ancho
1 teaspoon ground cumin
½ cup salsa and/or corn kernels, optional

Follow the Simple Tofu Scramble recipe. Add the bell pepper and jalapeño in with the onions and garlic. Add the remaining ingredients after cooking the tofu for 5 minutes.

"Buttermilk" Pancakes

We employed the pickiest pancake eaters we could find (Erica and Neil Greene) in order to develop the most authentic buttermilk pancake recipe possible. Buttermilk is really just sour milk with a fancy name. Seasoned bakers make their own buttermilk and you can too – without the milk! According to our pancake connoisseurs, the version made from the white wheat flour gets you those ultimately fluffy-licious flapjacks. Keeping the heat on low ensures the middle cooks all the way through without the outsides getting too browned.

Courtesy of *The 30 Minute Vegan*
Makes 10 to 12 pancakes

1½ cups soy milk
1 tablespoon + 1 teaspoon freshly squeezed lemon juice or raw apple cider vinegar
2 cups whole or white spelt flour (or substitute unbleached white wheat flour) (rice flour for gluten-free)
1 tablespoon + 1 teaspoon baking powder, sifted
½ teaspoon cinnamon
¼ cup plain soy yogurt
1 tablespoon safflower oil (or coconut oil)
2 tablespoons maple syrup
Earth Balance or coconut oil for cooking

1. Pour soy milk into a 2 cup measuring cup, add the lemon juice, stir gently, and allow it to sit out on the counter for 10 minutes.
2. Meanwhile, in a mixing bowl, sift the flour, baking powder, and cinnamon and whisk together. At this point, start to heat up your skillet or griddle. You may want to oil it as well. Keep the heat on low.
3. Add yogurt, oil, and maple syrup to the buttermilk and whisk

until well incorporated. Use a rubber spatula to combine the liquid with the flour mix. Stir until just blended, do not over mix.

4. Pour ¼ cup of the batter onto a lightly oiled surface over low heat. Do not try to spread the batter around. Just pour it on and it will spread out on its own. If it doesn't, you may need to add a little more soy milk to the batter (start with 2 tablespoons). Wait until the top is bubbly all the way through and flip. The pancakes are ready when you see steam coming out from the bottom and the bottom looks light brown. Enjoy with your favorite toppings and homemade syrup.

Variations

~ For blueberry, strawberry or raspberry pancakes, add ¾ cup fresh berries to the batter.

~ Add ½ cup dark chocolate chips to entertain the child in you.

~ Orange zest adds an uplifting effect. Start with 1 teaspoon. Lemon zest is nice as well, especially when you are adding blueberries. Or try orange raspberry.

~ For banana walnut pancakes, add ¾ cup diced banana and ¼ cup diced walnuts. You may also wish to add ¼ teaspoon of banana extract.

~ Flavor up your flapjacks with any of your favorite extracts and flavors such as vanilla, orange, or almond. Also try hazelnut, coconut or coffee!

Tips and Tricks

When adding ingredients to pancakes such as fruit and chocolate chips, it is advisable to leave these out of the actual batter and keep them in a bowl next to you while you are cooking. Pour the pancakes onto the griddle or pan and then sprinkle with your desired accoutrements. This is the best way to keep the pancakes from sticking and the fillings from burning. Things like zest and extracts can be added into the batter directly.

༄ BEVERAGES ༄

♥ Basic Nut Milk

Use this versatile recipe for all your plant based milk needs. Amazing on its own as a refreshing and nutritious beverage or in smoothies, baked goods, or any dish that calls for milk.

Courtesy of *The 30-Minute Vegan*
Makes 1 quart

 1 cup nut or seeds
 4 cups water

1. Rinse the nuts or seeds well and drain. If you have more time and for best results, see the chart at the end of the recipe for recommended soak times.
2. Place them in a blender with the water and blend on high speed for 30 seconds or until creamy.
3. Strain the milk through a fine mesh strainer, cheese cloth or mesh bag. If using a fine mesh strainer, use a spoon or rubber spatula to swirl the nut or seed meal around which allows the milk to drain faster.
4. If desired, sweeten with agave nectar or maple syrup to taste.

Variation
This recipe also works for rice milk. Just follow the ratios using uncooked brown rice and water. It's a convenient way to save on packaging; it's fresh and tastes better!

Nut, seed and rice milks will last for 3 to 4 days when stored in a glass jar in the refrigerator.

Nut & Seed Soaking Chart

For increased nutritional value and to enhance digestion, rinse nuts or seeds well and place them in a bowl or jar with water in a 1 part nut or seed to 3 or 4 part water ratio. Allow them to sit for the recommended time, covered at room temperature, before draining, rinsing, and using in recipes.

Nut/Seed	Soak Time in hours
Almonds	4 to 6
Brazil nuts	4 to 6
Cashews	1 to 2
Filberts (Hazel nuts)	4 to 6
Macadamia nuts	1 to 2
Pecans	4 to 6
Pine nuts	1 to 2
Pumpkin seeds	1 to 4
Sesame seeds	1 to 4
Sunflower seeds	1 to 4
Walnuts	4 to 6

↬ CONDIMENTS ↫

Vegan Sour Crème

Many times foods such as sour cream are the last to go for aspiring vegans. This recipe will help you take the plunge. So creamy and satisfying and when served with all of the fixings, you will never miss the dairy.

1 cup vegan mayonnaise such as Vegenaise or
home made (page 191)
1 tablespoon freshly squeezed lemon juice
Pinch dill, optional

Place all of the ingredients in a small bowl and whisk well. May be stored for up to 5 days in an airtight glass container in the refrigerator.

Garlic Herb Aioli

A flavorful spread that will take any of your wraps and sandwiches up to the next level. If you have time, make your own mayonnaise and use as the base (page 191).

Makes 1 cup

 1 cup Vegenaise, other non-dairy mayo or Vegan Mayonnaise
 1 to 2 garlic cloves, pressed or minced
 1 tablespoon minced Italian parsley
 ¾ teaspoon minced rosemary
 ½ teaspoon fresh thyme

Stir together all of the ingredients and store in an airtight container in the refrigerator for up to one week.

Variations
- For Chipotle Aioli, add 1 to 2 chipotle chiles, soaked until soft, seeded and minced.
- Add 2 teaspoon dehydrated onions and ½ teaspoon onion powder for a French Onion Dip.
- Try roasting the garlic cloves and then blending them together with the Vegenaise in a mini-food processor.

You can use pre-made vegan mayo (like Vegenaise) or you can make your own. Use this homemade mayo in all recipes that call for mayonnaise in the book. For best results, store in a glass container in the refrigerator and use within a week.

Vegan Mayonnaise

Ever made mayonnaise before? You will be surprised at how simple and delicious it is to prepare on your own and delighted that you can leave out the raw eggs.

Makes 2 ¼ cups

1 ½ cups safflower oil
¾ cup soy milk
½ teaspoon Dijon mustard
1 teaspoon agave nectar, optional
¾ teaspoon sea salt, or to taste
1 ½ teaspoon freshly squeezed lemon juice

1. Combine all of the ingredients except the lemon juice in a blender and blend until smooth.
2. Slowly add the lemon juice through the top while blending until the mixture thickens.

APPETIZERS, ⤳ SIDE DISHES ⤵ & SALADS

♥ Cashew Cheese Crudite

A simple plant-based cheese that can be used for spreads, wraps or as a dip for crudite. You can also use this cheese in casseroles such as lasagna or enchilada casseroles.

Courtesy of *Vegan Fusion World Cuisine*

1 batch Cashew Cheese
Assorted colorful vegetables such as carrot sticks, bell pepper slices, and celery sticks

Cashew Cheese

Makes 2 ½ cups

2 cups raw cashews
1 cup filtered water
⅓ cup red bell pepper, ribs and seeds removed, diced
2 ½ tablespoons green onion, diced
2 tablespoons fresh cilantro, minced
1 teaspoon garlic, minced, optional
1 teaspoon nama shoyu or wheat-free tamari, to taste
¼ teaspoon sea salt, to taste
Pinch crushed red pepper flakes

1. Blend cashews with water on high speed for 40-60 seconds until very smooth.

2. Place in a quart sized open-mouthed glass jar. Cover tightly with plastic wrap and secure with a rubber band. Cover with a towel and allow to sit in a warm place overnight.

3. Transfer cashew mixture into a large mixing bowl. Stir in red bell pepper, green onion, cilantro, garlic, if using, shoyu, salt and crushed red pepper.

4. Serve immediately or store in an airtight glass container in the fridge for 3-4 days. This recipe provides a great base for a variety of dips.

Variations

∾ Substitute macadamia nuts or pine nuts for the cashews and use other fresh herbs in place of the cilantro.

∾ Blend cashew mixture with red bell pepper before stirring in the other ingredients.

♥ Grilled Vegetable and Quinoa Salad

Courtesy of *Vegan Fusion Culinary Immersion*

Botanically classified as a seed, and commonly considered a grain, quinoa is a superfood of the ancient Incans of South America. It is high in protein and contains all essential amino acids. This is a simple recipe that can serve as a template for any vegetable and grain dish. You can replace the quinoa with any variety of rice, millet and even rice pasta. For the grilled vegetables, you can use the Maple Balsamic Marinade on the next page, or simply drizzle with oil, salt, and pepper before grilling. The vegetables can be raw, roasted or sauteed. Experiment with different herbs to create designer salads du jour.

Serves 6-8

3 ½ cups filtered water or stock

2 cups quinoa

¾ tsp sea salt

3 ½ cups assorted grilled vegetables, chopped (onion, bell peppers, zucchini, mushrooms, and or corn)

½ cup kalamata olives, sliced

½ cup green onion, sliced

¼ cup fresh herbs, minced (cilantro, oregano, basil, parsley, dill, mint or assortment)

2 tablespoons balsamic vinegar

1 tablespoon freshly squeezed lemon juice

½ teaspoon lemon zest

¼ tsp crushed red pepper flakes

Wheat-free tamari, sea salt and ground black pepper to taste

1. Place quinoa grain in large bowl and over with fresh cool water. Swish around and drain off the water. Repeat until water runs clear.

2. Place quinoa, salt, and water or stock in a 3 quart pan and bring to boil. Reduce heat to simmer, cover and cook until liquid is absorbed, approximately 10 minutes. (If quinoa is already prepared, use 5 ½ cups cooked quinoa for this recipe.) Place in a large bowl.

3. Place vegetables in the Balsamic Marinade (below) for 5 to 10 minutes, or lightly drizzle with oil, and salt and pepper. Grill vegetables and chop into small pieces. Add to bowl with quinoa and remaining ingredients and gently mix well.

Maple Balsamic Marinade

Use this simple marinade for grilled vegetables, or for roasting tofu or tempeh cutlets.

Makes approximately ¾ cup

    ¼ cup filtered water
    3 tablespoons wheat-free tamari or soy sauce
    2 tablespoons olive oil or coconut oil
    1 tablespoon maple syrup
    2 teaspoons balsamic vinegar
    1 teaspoon minced garlic or ginger
    Pinch cayenne pepper

Place all ingredients in a medium size bowl and whisk well.

Mixed Organic Green Salad with Tofu Feta and Green Goddess Dressing

Get creative with your salads – use colorful vegetables such as grated carrots and beets, chopped zucchini, thinly sliced purple cabbage, sprouts, toasted seeds and more. Top with the tofu feta and Goddess dressing to create a satisfying meal.

Serves 6

Assorted Mixed Salad Greens
Colorful Vegetables
1 recipe Tofu Feta (below)
1 recipe Green Goddess Dressing (next page)

1. Prepare the Tofu Feta
2. Prepare the Green Goddess Dressing
3. Arrange salad greens and colorful veggies in a serving bowl or on individual plates. Add crumbled Feta and drizzle with dressing.

Tofu Feta

14-ounces extra firm or super firm tofu, quartered
¼ cup freshly squeezed lemon juice
1 tablespoon miso paste
1 teaspoon minced fresh oregano
2 tablespoons minced flat-leaf parsley
½ teaspoon fresh thyme
½ teaspoon sea salt
¼ teaspoon ground black pepper

1. Place a steamer basket in a 3 quart pot with ½-inch of water over medium high heat. Place the tofu in the steamer basket, cover and cook for 5 minutes. Remove from the heat and run under cold water.

2. Meanwhile, place the remaining Tofu Feta ingredients in a small bowl and whisk well. Crumble the tofu into the bowl and stir well. Allow to sit for at least 5 minutes and up to overnight.

Garvin's Galactic Green Goddess

Courtesy of *Vegan Fusion World Cuisine*
Makes 2 ½ cups

⅔ cup soy or rice milk
1 cup vegan mayonnaise, Vegenaise brand or homemade (see page 191)
⅓ cup Basil, fresh, minced & tightly packed
2 tablespoons Italian parsley, fresh, minced
1 ½ tablespoons Apple cider vinegar, raw
1 ½ tablespoons wheat-free tamari or other soy sauce, to taste
¼ teaspoon ground black pepper
¼ teaspoon sea salt, or to taste
Pinch cayenne pepper

1. Place all of the ingredients in a blender and blend well.

Eggless Egg Salad

Nutritionally light years ahead of its animal product counterpart, this version uses tofu and vegan mayonnaise as the base. The spice turmeric gives it its distinctive yellow color. Delectable on sandwiches, wraps or in stuffed tomatoes.

Courtesy of *Vegan Fusion World Cuisine*
Serves 4

14 ounce Extra firm tofu, steamed, drained well and crumbled
¾ cup diced celery
½ cup diced red onion
½ cup Vegenaise or homemade vegan mayo (page 191)
1 tablespoon minced fresh dill
2 ½ teaspoons stone ground mustard
1 ½ teaspoons raw apple cider vinegar
1 teaspoon ground turmeric
½ teaspoon minced garlic
2½ tablespoons soy sauce
Black pepper, ground to taste
Sea salt, to taste

1. Combine all ingredients in a large mixing bowl and gently mix well. For additional flavor, allow to sit for a few hours before serving.

Charlie's Relief
Tuna-Free Tempeh Salad

Charlie is relieved we are opting for tempeh instead of fish in this remake of the classic salad. Serve in a sandwich or wrap with all of the fixings such as lettuce, tomato and onion. For a Tuna-free melt, stuff tomatoes with the salad and top with grated vegan cheese. Broil until the cheese is melted.

Courtesy of *Vegan Fusion World Cuisine*
Serves 4 to 6

1 pound soy tempeh, quartered

1 ¼ cups vegan mayonnaise such as Vegenaise or homemade (see page 191)

⅔ cup diced kosher dill pickles

½ cup diced celery

¼ cup diced red onion

2 tablespoons wheat-free tamari or other soy sauce, to taste

2 tablespoons minced Italian parsley

1 tablespoon stone ground mustard

2 teaspoons raw apple cider vinegar

½ teaspoon minced garlic

Sea salt, to taste

Black pepper, ground to taste

1. Chop the tempeh into ⅛-inch square pieces. Place in a steamer basket in a medium pot and steam for 10 minutes.

2. Remove the tempeh from the steamer basket, combine with the remaining ingredients in a large mixing bowl and mix well. For additional flavor, if you have more time, refrigerate for an hour before serving.

Vegan Cornbread

One of the most popular items at the Blossoming Lotus Restaurant on Kauai, this cornbread is a definite crowd pleaser. Wonderful on its own, served as a side with chili or soup, or with a Ranch Dipping Sauce (see page 202). Be sure to experiment with the variations!

Courtesy of *Vegan Fusion World Cuisine*
Makes one 9" x 13" cornbread

Dry
2 cups spelt flour, sifted well
⅞ cup corn meal
¾ cup millet
2½ tablespoons baking powder, sifted to remove lumps
¾ teaspoon sea salt

Wet
½ lb silken firm tofu,
1 ¾ cups water
¾ cup maple syrup
½ cup safflower oil

1. Preheat oven to 350°. Combine Dry ingredients in a large mixing bowl and whisk well. Add Wet ingredients to a blender and blend until creamy. Add wet to dry and mix well.
2. Pour into a parchment paper-lined 9" x 13" baking pan and bake until a toothpick comes out clean, approximately 45 minutes, or until top browns and cracks appear.

Variations

∞ Southwest: Add the following to dry mixture: ¼ cup ancho chilies, soaked in hot water, seeded and diced; ½ cup red bell pepper, diced; ¼ cup cilantro, minced; ½ cup corn, fresh or frozen.

∞ Blueberry or Strawberry: Add 1¼ cup of berries after all ingredients have been mixed together.

∞ Cranberry Walnut: Add 1 cup fresh cranberries and ½ cup chopped walnuts after all ingredients have been mixed together.

∞ Double Corn Bread: Add 1½ cup of corn after all ingredients have been mixed together.

Ranch Dipping Sauce or Dressing

We were surprised to learn that ranch dressing originated from a dude ranch in 1950's California, and that its actually one of the most popular dressings in the U.S. Sometimes you just want to smother your salad in a rich, creamy dressing. This is the one to choose. To turn this into a phenomenal Ranch dip or spread, leave out the soy milk.

Courtesy of *The 30-Minute Vegan*
Makes 1 ¼ cups

¾ cup Vegenaise (or other vegan mayo)
¼ cup soy milk or rice milk
2 tsp freshly squeezed lemon juice
2 tsp raw apple cider vinegar
1 garlic clove
2 tablespoons minced green onion, white part only
¼ teaspoon paprika, try smoked
¼ teaspoon sea salt
¼ teaspoon ground black pepper
½ teaspoon wheat-free tamari, or other soy sauce, to taste
Pinch of cayenne
1 tablespoon minced Italian parsley

1. Blend all of the ingredients except the parsley until creamy. Pour into a small bowl. Add the parsley, stir well and enjoy.
2. This dressing will thicken if left in the fridge. Re-blend or whisk in some additional soy milk to return it to a pourable consistency.

Variations
∿ Replace the parsley with an equal amount of dill.
∿ Add 2 teaspoons nutritional yeast for a cheesy flavor.

ᘓ SOUPS ᘏ

♥ Creamy Corn Soup

This is a silky soup that replicates the popular Chinese food restaurant dish. Adding the optional grated tofu creates the egg-like texture that is included in most versions. We blend the corn with soy milk to create the 'creamed corn' effect.

Courtesy of *The 30 Minute Vegan's Taste of the East*
Serves 4 to 6

> 1 tablespoon toasted sesame oil
>
> 1 small onion, chopped small (1 ¼ cups)
>
> 3 cloves of garlic, pressed or minced
>
> 2 cups vegetable stock or 2 cups water plus 1 tablespoon soy sauce
>
> 1 pound bag frozen corn or 3 cups fresh
>
> 2 cups soy milk
>
> 1 teaspoon sea salt or to taste
>
> ½ teaspoon 5-spice powder
>
> ¼ teaspoon white or ground black pepper, or to taste
>
> ¾ cup grated extra firm tofu, optional
>
> 1 tablespoon mirin, optional
>
> Pinch cayenne
>
> 1 tablespoon arrowroot dissolved in ½ cup cold water
>
> ¼ cup diced green onion

1. Place the oil in a medium pot over medium high heat. Add the onion and garlic and cook for 3 minutes, stirring frequently. Add 1 cup of stock and 2 cups of corn and cook for 3 minutes, stirring occasionally. Transfer the contents to a blender and carefully blend with 1 cup of soy milk.

2. Return to the pot and add the remaining stock, soy milk, and cup of corn. Add all of the other ingredients except the arrowroot mixture and green onion. Cook over low heat for 10 minutes, stirring occasionally.

3. Add the arrowroot mixture and stir until soup slightly thickens. Cook for an additional 5 minutes. Garnish with the green onion before serving.

Variations

∾ Replace the corn with vegetables such as broccoli, cauliflower or zucchini.

∾ Replace the soy milk with rice or almond milk.

♥ Raw Carrot Brazil Nut Soup

Enjoying foods in their raw state provides you with a maximum amount of nutrients. Using this recipe as a template, you can replace the carrot juice with a vegetable juice of your choosing. Replace the Brazil nuts with macadamia nuts or cashews. Experiment with different herbs and spices and discover the bounty of culinary delights possible with raw soups.

Courtesy of *Vegan Fusion Culinary Immersion*
Serves 4

3 ½ cups carrot juice, fresh (approx. 3 1/2 lbs carrots)
¼ cup Brazil nuts, soaked
¼ cup avocado, mashed
1 tablespoon peeled and minced ginger
1 clove garlic
1 tablespoon lemon juice, fresh squeezed
1 tablespoons wheat-free tamari (optional)
2 tablespoons fresh mined Italian parsley
1 teaspoon seeded and diced jalapeno pepper
2 tablespoons thinly sliced green onion Pinch crushed red pepper flakes
Sea salt, to taste
Black pepper, ground to taste

Raw Creme Fraiche

½ cup cashews, soaked in a few cups of water for 45 minutes or longer
½ cups water
2 teaspoons freshly squeezed lemon juice
Sea salt to taste

1. Prepare the soup by placing all ingredients except parsley, red pepper flakes, salt, pepper and cashews in a blender and blend until smooth. Transfer to a large bowl.

2. Add the parsley, red pepper flakes, salt and pepper and stir well.

3. Prepare the Creme Fraiche by draining the cashews and rinsing well. Blend with water and lemon juice, transfer to a small bowl and add salt to taste.

4. Serve soup with a dollop of the Creme Fraiche.

♥ Broccoli Bisque with Shiitake Mushrooms

Ode to creamy and rich vegan soups. By blending the soup with nuts such as macadamia, cashew, or pine nut we create a creaminess that will leave your guests wondering "where's the dairy"? Adding the diced shiitake mushrooms and the sea vegetable arame creates a chowder effect that is sure to please. This is another template recipe where many variations are possible.

Courtesy of *Vegan Fusion Culinary Immersion*
Serves 4

¼ cup arame soaked in ¾ cup hot water
3 tablespoons olive oil
1 medium onion, chopped (1 1/2 cups)
¾ cup celery, sliced thin
2 tablespoons garlic, minced
5 cups water or vegetable stock
4 cups broccoli flowerets
1 cup macadamia nuts, roasted
1 cup chopped shiitake mushrooms
2 teaspoons sea salt, or to taste
1 tablespoon dill, fresh minced (1 teaspoon dry)
¼ teaspoon crushed red pepper flakes
Black pepper, ground to taste
Wheat-free tamari or other soy sauce to taste (optional)

1. Soak the arame in the hot water.
2. Add oil to a 3 quart pot and cook on medium heat for 1 minute. Add onion, celery and garlic, and cook for 3 minutes, stirring frequently. Add water or stock, and broccoli, and cook until all

veggies are just soft, approximately 20 minutes, stirring occasionally. Remove from heat.

3. Meanwhile, place 1 tablespoon of oil in a small saute pan over medium high heat. Add the shiitake mushrooms and cook for 5 minutes, stirring frequently and adding small amounts of water or vegetable stock if necessary to prevent sticking.

4. Transfer the soup to a blender (we recommend a Vita-Mix), add macadamia nuts and very carefully blend until smooth. Blend in batches, being careful to fill blender only half full. Start with low speed initially; slowly increase speed until desired consistency is reached. Return to pot, add remaining ingredients, including the sauteed shiitakes, the arame and the arame soak water, and stir well.

Variations

ᐁ Hearty Broccoli Bisque: Add ¾ cup of corn or ¾ cup coarsely chopped broccoli after blending for more of a textured soup. Allow broccoli to cook through before serving.

ᐁ Cauliflower Bisque: Substitute cauliflower for broccoli and add 3 tablespoon of nutritional yeast before blending.

ᐁ Creamy Vegetable: Replace broccoli with other veggies like zucchini or corn for a creamy vegetable soup.

ᐁ Replace the macadamia nuts with cashews or blanched almonds. Experiment with different herbs.

♥ Mahatma's Mung Dahl

Dahl is an ancient soup popular in Indian cuisine made with various legumes such as lentils, split peas or mung beans. This is a simple soup recipe template. You can replace the mung beans with legumes of your choosing. You can also add 1 cup of finely chopped vegetables such as zucchini, cabbage, broccoli flowerets or your favorites. Enjoy with a dollop of Vegan Sour Cream (page 189), a bowl of rice and a yummy mixed salad for a meal fit for a yogi.

Courtesy of *Vegan Fusion World Cuisine*
5 - 6 servings

6 cups vegetable stock or water
1 cup mung beans, sorted & rinsed well
1 medium onion diced
1 medium carrot, cubed
½ cup celery, thinly sliced
1 tablespoon minced garlic
1 tablespoon peeled & minced ginger
1 tablespoon seeded & minced jalapeño,
⅓ cup wheat-free tamari or other soy sauce, to taste
1 tablespoon cumin seed, optionally toasted in a dry saute pan until golden brown
1 teaspoon cumin powder, optionally toasted in a dry saute pan until golden brown
½ teaspoon curry powder
¼ teaspoon sea salt, to taste
¼ teaspoon ground black pepper, to taste
Pinch cayenne pepper
2 tablespoons minced cilantro, minced

1. Rinse beans and place in a medium sized pot with 6 cups of stock on medium high heat. Add onion, carrot, celery, garlic, ginger and jalapeño, cook on medium high heat until beans are soft, approximately 30 minutes, stirring occasionally.

2. Add the tamari and remaining ingredients, except cilantro, and cook for an additional 5 minutes, stirring occasionally.

3. Add cilantro, remove from heat and enjoy

You can rinse and soak the beans overnight or for several hours beforehand to improve digestibility

✌ENTREES ✌

Grilled Tempeh Reuben with Thousand Island Dressing

Popular throughout diners nationwide, this vegan version makes use of tempeh – a cultured soy product that has a higher nutritional profile than its sibling – tofu. If no grill is available, you can saute or roast the tempeh. You can also substitute the tempeh with extra firm tofu cutlets or even portobello mushrooms.

Courtesy of *Vegan Fusion Culinary Immersion*
Serves 2

> 1 tablespoons wheat-free tamari or other soy sauce
>
> 1 tablespoon olive oil
>
> 1 tablespoon water
>
> ⅛ teaspoon chipotle chile powder, optional
>
> 1 teaspoon maple syrup
>
> 8 oz Tempeh, sliced in half into two thin cutlets
>
> ¼ cup Thousand Island Dressing (below)
>
> 2 tablespoons Sauerkraut
>
> 2 Spelt buns or 4 slices whole grain rye bread
>
> Grated vegan cheese (Daiya or Follow Your Heart brand), optional but recommended
>
> Sliced red onion, tomato or fixings of choice

Grill: Preheat grill. Place the soy sauce, olive oil, water, maple syrup and chipotle chile powder in a casserole dish and whisk well. Add the tempeh and allow to marinate for 10 minutes or longer, flipping once or twice to ensure even coating. Cook until grill marks appear on both sides and tempeh is cooked thoroughly, approximately 10 minutes, brushing cutlets with marinade sauce periodically.

No Grill: If no grill is available, cutlets can be sautéed in 2 tablespoons of oil until golden brown, approximately 8 minutes, or placed in the marinade on a well oiled baking sheet and baked in a 375° oven until golden brown, approximately 15 minutes.

Slice buns in half and toast on grill until warmed. Add your favorite fixings.

Thousand Island Dressing

Makes approximately 1 ½ cups

½ cup Vegenaise
½ cup Catsup
¼ cup finely diced kosher dill pickles, or relish
1 teaspoon minced garlic
½ teaspoon minced fresh dill

Combine all ingredients in a large mixing bowl and mix well.

♥ BBQ Tempeh Sandwich

Another sandwich that will become a favorite in your household. Make extra sauce and use as a topping for steamed or roasted vegetables.

Courtesy of *Vegan Fusion Culinary Immersion*
Serves 4

Two 8-ounce packages tempeh – cut into 4 cutlets
2 tablespoons soy sauce
1 tablespoon water
1 tablespoon olive or coconut oil
8 slices whole grain bread or other bread of choice
8 lettuce leaves
1 large tomato, sliced
4 red onion slices
1 recipe BBQ Sauce (see below)

BBQ Sauce

Makes 1 ½ cups

1 cup ketchup
3 tablespoons molasses or barley malt syrup, or 2 tablespoons maple syrup
½ teaspoon garlic powder
¼ teaspoon liquid smoke
1 teaspoon chile powder (try chipotle)
1 ½ teaspoons raw apple cider vinegar
2 tablespoons olive oil
3 tablespoons water
1 teaspoon Dijon or stone ground mustard

1. Preheat the oven to 350°F. Place the soy sauce, water and oil in a small dish and add the tempeh cutlets. Allow to marinate for 5 minutes, flipping a few times to evenly coat.

2. Place the tempeh and the marinade ingredients on a baking sheet and cook for 5 minutes. Flip, and cook for an additional 10 minutes.

3. While the tempeh is baking, prepare the BBQ sauce by combining all of the ingredients in a large mixing bowl and whisking well. Pour some sauce over the tempeh while it is baking.

4. When the tempeh is finished cooking, place the cutlet on the sandwich with the remaining ingredients and as much BBQ sauce as you wish. You can store the extra sauce in a glass container in the refrigerator for up to 5 days.

Variations

∾ Replace the tempeh with an equal amount of extra firm tofu.

∾ Try serving on toasted sourdough, rye bread, or an artisan bread such as olive rosemary.

∾ Add 1 tablespoon of minced garlic or peeled and minced ginger to the tempeh marinade. For BBQ Sauce: if you don't have ketchup, replace it with one 6-ounce can of tomato paste and ¼ cup water.

∾ Caramelize 1 cup of thinly sliced onions in a saute pan by sauteing in oil over low heat for 20 to 30 minutes, stirring occasionally and adding small amounts of water if necessary to prevent sticking. Add BBQ sauce and cook for 5 minutes over low heat before serving.

♥ Quiche Monet

Real men eat vegan quiche! This dish is an offshoot of the famous Quiche Lorraine, which typically contains bacon and eggs, this heart healthy quiche was inspired by a trip to Monet's gardens at Giverny and uses tofu to create the body of the dish.

Courtesy of *The 30 Minute Vegan's Taste of Europe*
Serves 4 to 6

One 9-inch vegan pie crust (go for spelt if you can)
1 tablespoon oil
1 ¼ cups sliced leeks, rinsed and drained very well
3 garlic cloves, pressed or minced
½ cup chanterelle or shiitake mushrooms, diced
4-ounces fakin bakin (¾ cup diced)
2 packages 12.3-ounces silken tofu
2 tablespoons soy, rice, or almond milk
2 tablespoons nutritional yeast
2 tablespoons tahini
1 tablespoon freshly squeezed lemon juice
¾ teaspoon sea salt, or to taste
⅛ teaspoon ground black pepper
¼ teaspoon cayenne pepper
1 tablespoon finely chopped tarragon
1 teaspoon dry marjoram or 1 tablespoon fresh minced
½ cup grated vegan cheese, optional

1. Preheat the oven to 450°F. Poke a few holes in the pie shell with a fork and bake for 10 minutes. Remove from the oven.

2. Meanwhile, place a large sauté pan over medium high heat. Add the oil, leeks, and garlic and cook for 2 minutes, stirring

constantly. Add the mushrooms and fakin bacon, and cook for 3 minutes stirring frequently.

3. Place the tofu, soy milk, nutritional yeast, tahini, lemon juice, salt, pepper, and cayenne in a food processor and process until creamy. Transfer to the sauté pan with the remaining ingredients and mix well.

4. Pour into the pie shell and bake for 10 minutes. Reduce the heat to 425°F and bake for an additional 10 minutes. Serve warm or cold.

Variations

∽ Replace chanterelle mushrooms with shiitake, oyster, or crimini.

∽ Add 1 tablespoon Herbes de Provence.

∽ Add 1 cup chopped spinach along with mushrooms.

♥ Mixed Vegetable Korma

Korma is a creamy dish of North Indian/Pakistani origin. *Korma* traditionally refers to a cooking style that involves braising. Nowadays it generally refers to a curry dish with a cream-based sauce or gravy. Our version is a crowd-pleasing and hearty dish, best enjoyed with basmati rice or quinoa.

Courtesy of *The 30 Minute Vegan's Taste of the East*
Serves 6

¾ cup chopped cashews, raw or roasted
2 cups soy creamer or soy milk
2 tablespoons sesame or coconut oil
1 teaspoon ground coriander
1 teaspoon ground cumin
½ teaspoon curry powder
1 onion, diced (1 ¼ cups)
2 large cloves garlic, pressed or minced
2 teaspoons seeded and diced hot chile or ½ teaspoon crushed red pepper flakes
4 ½ cups assorted colorful veggies such as small broccoli and/or cauliflower flowerets, diced red bell peppers, thinly sliced carrots or your favorites
¾ cup water
¼ cup coconut milk (regular or light) or unsweetened vegan yogurt, optional
2 teaspoons poppy seeds
¾ teaspoon garam masala
½ teaspoon chile powder
⅛ teaspoon turmeric powder
Pinch cinnamon
1 tablespoon wheat-free tamari or other soy sauce, to taste
¾ teaspoon sea salt, or to taste
2 tablespoons minced fresh cilantro

1. Place ½ cup of the cashews and 1 cup of the soy creamer in a blender and blend until creamy.

2. Place the oil in a large sauté pan or wok over medium-high heat. Add the coriander, cumin, and curry, and cook for 1 minute, stirring constantly. Add the onion, garlic, and chile, and cook for 3 minutes, stirring frequently. Reduce the heat to medium, add the contents of the blender, as well as the veggies, water, and remaining soy creamer, and cook for 10 minutes, stirring occasionally.

3. Add the remaining cashews, and all of the other remaining ingredients, except the cilantro and cook for an additional 5 minutes, gently stirring occasionally. Add the cilantro and mix well before serving.

Variations

∽ Replace the cauliflower with broccoli, cabbage, potatoes, or other vegetables of your choosing.

∽ You can toast the cashews if you wish.

∽ You can replace 1 cup of the assorted veggies with 8 ounces of tempeh, or extra firm tofu cubes cut into ½-inch cubes. To do so, preheat the oven or toaster oven to 375°F. Place the tempeh, 2 tablespoons soy sauce, and 1 tablespoon of the sesame oil on a small baking sheet and stir well to evenly coat the tempeh. Place in the oven and bake for 10 minutes. Add to the pot along with the cashews.

♥ Indonesian Seitan Satay over Indonesian Coconut Rice

Originating in Indonesia and making its way across South East Asia, satay is a popular dish across all borders. Typically served on skewers with a spicy dipping sauce, our version replaces the meat with marinated seitan. Turmeric is traditionally used to impart a yellow color to the dish.

Courtesy of *The 30 Minute Vegan's Taste of the East*
Makes 4 appetizer portions

Seitan Satay

8-ounce package seitan

1 tablespoon sesame or peanut oil

1 cup sliced onion

2 cloves garlic, pressed or minced

⅛ teaspoon turmeric powder

2 teaspoon wheat-free tamari or soy sauce

2 teaspoon rice vinegar

1 cup or more Peanut Sauce

4 bamboo or other skewers

1. Slice the seitan into approximately 16 equal sized pieces.
2. Heat the oil in a sauté pan over medium high heat. Add the onions and garlic, and cook for 2 minutes, stirring frequently. Add the seitan and turmeric, and cook for 10 minutes, stirring occasionally. Add the tamari and vinegar, stir well and reduce the heat to low.
3. Prepare the peanut sauce by following the recipe below. Pour into a small bowl.

4. Place 4 pieces of seitan on each skewer and serve with the sauce. You can serve the onions along side the skewers or place some on top of each skewer.

Variations

ℛ Try grilling the seitan and the onion.

ℛ For a gluten free version, replace the seitan with marinated and roasted tempeh or tofu.

ℛ You can add 1 inch slices of red, green, and yellow bell pepper, as well as mushrooms and create the kebab of your dreams!

Peanut Sauce

Makes 2 1/2 cups sauce

½ tablespoon sesame or peanut oil

1 ½ tablespoon minced shallot or onion

1 cloves garlic, pressed or minced

1 teaspoon peeled and minced ginger

½ teaspoon seeded and diced jalapeño or other hot pepper

½ cup coconut milk, regular or light

¼ cup + 2 tablespoon water

½ cup crunchy peanut butter

½ tablespoon maple syrup, organic brown sugar or sweetener of choice

2 teaspoon wheat-free tamari or soy sauce, or to taste

¾ teaspoon tamarind paste or 1 tablespoon freshly squeezed lime juice

¼ teaspoon sea salt

Crushed red pepper flakes to taste

1. Place the oil in a pot with the sesame oil over medium heat.

2. Add the shallot, garlic, ginger and jalapeño and cook for 3 minutes, stirring frequently.

3. Reduce the heat to low, add the remaining ingredients, stirring occasionally.

4. Pour the sauce into a bowl.

Variation:

∾ Replace the peanut butter with almond butter

Indonesian Coconut Rice

This dish packs a punch of flavor and boasts a winning combination of rice, coconut milk, lemongrass, and hot chiles.

Courtesy of *The 30 Minute Vegan's Taste of the East*
Serves 6 to 8

4 lemongrass stalks, bottoms and outer stalks removed

2 cups white basmati rice

1 (14-ounce) can coconut milk, regular or light

1 ¾ cups water

1 ¾ teaspoons sea salt, or to taste

1 tablespoon sesame oil

3 cloves garlic, pressed or minced

2 tablespoons peeled and minced fresh ginger

1 cup sliced green onions

1 teaspoon ground cloves

¼ teaspoon crushed red pepper flakes, or to taste

½ cup shredded unsweetened coconut or coconut flakes, toasted

1. Crush the lemongrass by lightly pounding it with a wooden spoon or other heavy object. Place them in a large pot with rice, coconut milk, water, and salt, and bring to a boil over

high heat. Reduce the heat to simmer, cover, and cook until all of the liquid is absorbed, approximately 15 minutes. Remove from the heat.

2. Meanwhile, place the sesame oil in a large sauté pan over medium heat. Add the garlic, ginger, and green onions and cook for 3 minutes, stirring frequently. Add the remaining ingredients except the toasted coconut and cook for 2 minutes, stirring frequently.

3. When the rice is done cooking, combine all of the ingredients in a large mixing bowl and gently mix well. Remove the lemongrass stalks and garnish with toasted coconut before serving.

Variations

∾ Add 2 cups diced vegetables, such as red bell peppers, mushrooms, or celery, to the sauté pan along with the green onions.

∾ Replace the basmati rice with brown rice, or even with quinoa. Use 2 cups of quinoa and 4 cups of total liquid for this recipe.

♥ Fettuccini Alfredo

Talk about successful self promotion! Alfredo di Lelio, a Roman chef in the early 1900's, named a cheese and butter pasta dish after himself and the rest is history. What would Alfredo say about the vegan revolution that has swept the culinary world and veganized his prized creation? I'll let you be the judge after tasting this rich and satisfying dish.

Courtesy of *The 30 Minute Vegan's Taste of Europe*
Serves 4 to 6

28 ounces brown rice pasta, such as fettucini, linguini
or spaghetti
¾ teaspoon salt, optional

Alfredo Sauce

3 cups soy milk
½ cup cashews (¾ cup if not using the vegan cheese)
1/4 cup nutritional yeast
1 large garlic clove
2 teaspoons wheat-free tamari or other soy sauce
1 teaspoon sea salt, to taste
¼ teaspoon ground black pepper
¼ teaspoon crushed red pepper flakes
2 tablespoons freshly squeezed lemon juice
1 ¼ cup grated vegan cheese, mozzarella style, optional
(but your friends will thank you if you add it)
3 tablespoons chiffonade basil
2 tablespoons finely chopped flat-leaf parsley
½ cup finely chopped green onion

1. Bring a covered large pot of water to boil on high heat. Remove the cover, add the pasta, and salt, if using, and cook according to package instructions. Drain well.

2. Meanwhile, prepare the sauce. Place the soy milk, cashews, nutritional yeast, garlic, soy sauce, salt, pepper, and crushed red pepper flakes, in a blender and blend until creamy. Transfer to a pot and place on medium heat. Cook for 5 minutes, stirring frequently.

3. Reduce the heat to low, add the lemon juice, and vegan cheese, if using, and cook for 5 minutes stirring occasionally. Add the basil and parsley and mix well.

4. Combine the pasta and sauce in a large bowl and gently mix well. Top with the green onion before serving.

Variations
ɑ‍ Add 1 teaspoon fresh oregano, and ½ teaspoon each of thyme, minced sage, and minced rosemary.

♥ Mediterranean Pistachio Crusted Tofu with Saffron Quinoa Pilaf

I am excited to share this recipe, which, along with the Saffron Quinoa Pilaf, is the winner of Vegan.com's 2011 "Recipe of the Year" award. This is a recipe to prepare when you want to impress folks with the wonderful culinary potential of tofu. It is a creative and colorful dish with several layers of delicious flavor and amazing texture that lends itself to many variations. Since tomatoes figure prominently in the topping, be sure to choose the freshest ones possible for the most auspicious results. Serve with the Saffron Quinoa Pilaf (page 228).

Courtesy of Vegan.com
Serves 4

Tofu

14-ounces extra firm tofu

2 tablespoons wheat-free tamari or other soy sauce

1 tablespoon olive oil or your favorite, optional

1 tablespoon water

Tahini Marinade

2 tablespoons sesame tahini

1 teaspoon wheat-free tamari or other soy sauce

1 teaspoon freshly squeezed lemon juice

2 tablespoons water, or more depending on consistency of tahini

Crust

¾ cup roasted, unsalted pistachio nuts

1 tablespoon minced flat-leaf parsley, basil, or herb of your choosing

½ teaspoon dried oregano

¼ teaspoon dried thyme

¼ teaspoon crushed red pepper flakes

⅛ teaspoon sea salt, or to taste

⅛ teaspoon ground black pepper

Mediterranean Vegetables

¾ cup chopped artichoke hearts, chopped

1 ½ cups chopped tomatoes (½-inch chop)

½ cup finely chopped arugula or spinach

3 tablespoons finely chopped Kalamata olives

2 tablespoons diced green onion

1 tablespoon thinly sliced or shaved, and chopped fennel

1 tablespoon capers

2 tablespoons chiffonade basil

2 teaspoons fresh minced oregano or ½ teaspoon dried

½ teaspoon fresh thyme or ¼ teaspoon dried

¼ teaspoon lemon zest

Dressing

2 tablespoons olive oil

1 tablespoon freshly squeezed lemon juice

2 teaspoons balsamic vinegar

1 garlic clove, pressed or minced

¼ teaspoon sea salt, or to taste

¼ teaspoon ground black pepper

1. Preheat the oven or toaster oven to 375°F. Place the soy sauce, olive oil, if using, and water on a baking dish and stir well. Slice the tofu into 4 cutlets and place in the baking dish. Marinate for at least 5 minutes or up to 30 minutes, flipping periodically.

2. While the tofu is marinating, prepare the tahini marinade by placing the ingredients in a small bowl and whisking well. You are looking for a smooth, spreadable consistency. Since the consistency of tahini varies greatly, you may need to add a bit more water.

3. Place the tofu, along with its marinade, in the oven and roast for 10 minutes. While the tofu is cooking, prepare the crust. Pulse chop the pistachio nuts in a food processor until they are coarse crumbs. Be careful not to over-process or it will turn into a paste. Transfer to a bowl with the remaining crust ingredients and mix well.

4. Meanwhile, combine the topping ingredients in a mixing bowl and gently mix well. Combine the dressing ingredients in a small bowl and stir well. Add to the topping and gently mix well.

5. Remove the tofu from the oven and coat the top of the cutlets with tahini marinade, using a spoon. Liberally top the cutlets with the crust mixture and bake for an additional 10 minutes.

6. To serve, slice the cutlets into triangles and top with the Mediterranean Vegetables. Serve over a bed of arugula and alongside the Saffron Quinoa Pilaf.

Variations

∾ So many are possible. You can replace the tofu with tempeh, Portobello mushrooms, or eggplant or zucchini steaks.

∾ All or a portion of the pistachio nuts can be replaced with macadamia nuts, walnuts, pecans, or cashews.

∾ Try adding 3 tablespoons dried coconut to the crust mixture.

∾ Experiment with your favorite spices and herbs.

∾ Feel free to increase the quantity of fennel, olives, garlic, or herbs, depending on your preferences.

Saffron Quinoa Pilaf

Creating a pilaf by adding vegetables and herbs to a grain is a simple way to take the flavor of your dish to the next level. The saffron adds a beautiful color and unique dimension to the quinoa. If saffron is not available, feel free to leave it out – you will still have a lovely pilaf to compliment the Mediterranean Pistachio Tofu Cutlets (page 225).

Serves 4 to 6

1 ¼ cups quinoa, rinsed and drained well
2 ¼ cups vegetable stock or water
½ teaspoon sea salt, to taste
½ teaspoon saffron threads
¼ cup thinly sliced green onion
1 tablespoon freshly squeezed lemon juice
½ teaspoon lightly packed lemon zest, optional
2 to 3 tablespoons finely chopped flat-leaf parsley or chiffonade basil

1. Place the quinoa, vegetable stock, salt, and saffron threads in a pot over high heat. Bring to a boil.
2. Cover, reduce the heat to low, and simmer until all liquid is absorbed, about 15 minutes. Allow to sit for 5 minutes longer.
3. Add the remaining ingredients and gently mix well.

To serve, place quinoa in a ramekin, ring mold, or 1 cup measuring cup and press firmly down. Flip on to each serving plate before adding Pistachio Tofu and Mediterranean Vegetables.

Variations

ᵔ Add ½ cup nuts such as pine nuts or slivered almonds or chopped walnuts, pistachios, or pecans after cooking.

ᵔ Add ¼ cup dried fruit like currants or cranberries after cooking.

ᵔ Add 1 teaspoon lemon zest after cooking.

ᵔ Replace the saffron with 1 teaspoon of grated fresh turmeric.

The Good Shepherd's Pie with Mushroom Onion Gravy

In "The Good Shepherd's Pie," the shepherd is good because he is allowing his flock to roam in peace and not including them in his meal. This hearty dish clearly proves that vegan meals can be delicious and filling. If you wish, you can place the casserole into pre-made pie crusts.

Courtesy of *Vegan Fusion World Cuisine*
45 min prep / 1 hour 10 min cooking / 9" x 13" casserole, serves 6 to 8

Shepherd's Pie

10-12 medium Potatoes, ½" cubes (approximately 12 cups), try Yukon gold

28 ounces extra firm tofu, crumbled

1 cup coconut, rice or soy milk

¾ cup diced yellow onion

¾ cup carrots, ½" cubes

¾ cup peas

¾ cup corn, fresh or frozen

½ cup thinly sliced celery

½ cup diced red bell pepper

½ cup thinly sliced mushrooms, try shiitake or crimini

¼ cup tahini

2 tablespoons olive oil

2 tablespoons minced garlic

2 tablespoons minced fresh basil (1 tablespoon dry)

2 tablespoon minced Italian parsley

4 teaspoons wheat-free tamari, or other soy sauce, to taste (optional)

2 teaspoons maple syrup or barley malt syrup, optional

1 ½ teaspoons sea salt, to taste

1 teaspoon fresh thyme (½ teaspoon dry)

2 teaspoons minced fresh sage (1 teaspoon dry)

½ teaspoon ground black pepper

½ teaspoon crushed red pepper flakes

¼ teaspoon cayenne pepper, to taste

1. Preheat oven to 350°. Place potatoes in a large pot with filtered water. Bring to a boil and cook until potatoes are soft, approximately 15 minutes. Drain well, place in a large mixing bowl with coconut milk and mash well. Add salt and pepper to taste. Set aside.

2. While potatoes are cooking, place oil in a large sauté pan on medium high heat. Add onion and garlic, cook for 3 minutes, stirring frequently. Add carrots, celery, bell pepper and mushrooms, cook for 10 minutes, stirring frequently. Add water if necessary to prevent sticking. Add tofu and cook for 5 minutes, stirring frequently. Place in a large mixing bowl with remaining ingredients except potatoes and mix well.

3. Place tofu vegetable mixture in a well oiled 9" x 13" casserole dish. Top with mashed potatoes, using a spatula to create a smooth surface. Score pretty designs on top with a fork. Bake until slightly golden brown and completely cooked, approximately 25 minutes. Cool for 10-15 minutes.

Serving suggestions

～ Serve with Mushroom Onion Gravy (see next page) and a dollop of non-dairy Sour Crème.

Variations

～ Potato layer may be placed on the bottom, topped with the tofu layer. Once refrigerated, this creates a more solid foundation, and allows for different sized pieces to be cut and served individually.

∾ You can also replace all or some of the potatoes with yams or sweet potatoes.

∾ Go crazy and replace 2 cups of the potatoes with parsnips.

∾ Replace the peas, carrots and corns with an equal amount of your favorite vegetables.

Mushroom Onion Gravy

This recipe may become your new best friend and is the height of vegan comfort food. In addition to topping the Shepherd's pie, you can serve over mashed potatoes, roasted vegetables, or tempeh or tofu cutlets. Nutritional yeast is a key ingredient here. It's an amazing source of vegan protein and B-vitamins, imparts a nutty and cheesy flavor to dishes.

Courtesy of *Vegan Fusion Culinary Immersion*
Makes 4 cups

¼ cup spelt or gluten-free flour
¼ cup + 1 tablespoon safflower oil
1 ½ cups onion, half moon slices
2 tablespoons garlic, minced
1 cup thinly sliced shiitake mushrooms
2 ½ cups water or veggie stock
¼ cup nutritional yeast
¼ cup wheat-free tamari or other soy sauce, to taste
2 tablespoons finely chopped Italian parsley
½ teaspoon fresh ground black pepper
Sea salt – to taste

1. Create a roux by combining spelt flour and ¼ cup oil in a small bowl and whisking well.

2. Place remaining tablespoon of oil in a saucepan on medium high heat. Add onion, garlic and mushrooms, and cook until onions are translucent, approximately 5 minutes, stirring frequently. Add water, nutritional yeast, soy sauce and sage, and bring to a boil, stirring frequently. Reduce heat to simmer, add roux and stir constantly until sauce thickens. Add salt and pepper to taste.

Serving suggestions

∾ Serve over mashed potatoes, pasta, rice, tofu or tempeh cutlets

Variations

∾ Try replacing parsley with other fresh minced herbs like sage, dill or basil.

∾ You can also create the roux by cooking the flour and oil over high heat for a few minutes until the flour browns this will impart a rich flavor and darker color to your gravy.

♥ Spanikopita

Who says vegans can't have a plate smashing good time? Here is a vegan take on a traditional Greek dish made with phyllo dough and Feta Cheese. Serve with Mushroom Onion Gravy (page 231) or Green Goddess Dressing and a dollop of Vegan Sour Cream (page 189).

Courtesy of *Vegan Fusion World Cuisine*
1 hour prep / 40 min cooking / 9"x13" casserole dish

   28 ounces extra firm tofu, crumbled

   1 package phyllo sheets, spelt variety if possible

   6 cups spinach, rinsed well

   2 cups diced onion

   2 tablespoons olive oil

   ¾ cup garbanzo beans, cooked, drained & mashed

   ¾ cup roasted creamy tahini

   ½ cup diced Kalamata olives

   ¼ cup minced garlic

   ¼ cup wheat-free tamari or other soy sauce, to taste

   3 tablespoons finely chopped Italian parsley

   2 tablespoons finely chopped fresh basil

   2 tablespoons nutritional yeast

   2 teaspoons minced fresh oregano (or 1 teaspoon dry)

   1 ½ teaspoons fresh thyme (or ¾ teaspoon dry)

   1 teaspoon minced fresh rosemary

   ¾ teaspoon sea salt, or to taste

   ½ teaspoon ground black pepper, to taste

   ¼ cup corn, coconut, or olive oil for basting

1. Steam spinach lightly for 3-5 minutes and drain well.

2. Preheat oven to 350°. Place 2 tablespoons of oil in a large pot on medium high heat. Add onions and garlic, cook 5 minutes, stirring frequently. Add the tofu and cook for 10 minutes, stirring frequently. Add the remaining ingredients, except the phyllo dough and corn oil, cook an additional 5 minutes, stirring frequently. Remove from heat.

3. Lightly oil a 9"x13" casserole dish. Place ⅓ of the phyllo dough (7 sheets) on the bottom of the dish, one sheet at a time, lightly oiling each sheet with corn or olive oil using a small pastry brush. Place half of the tofu mixture on top of the phyllo dough.

4. Repeat step 2, using 7 sheets of the phyllo dough and the remaining ½ of the tofu mixture. Top with the remaining phyllo dough, lightly brush with oil, and bake until phyllo is golden brown, approximately 20 minutes. Allow to cool 10-15 minutes before serving.

ꙩ DESSERTS ꙩ

Mint Chocolate Chip Cookies

Desserts are at the forefront of the vegan revolution as they are so easy to prepare without eggs and dairy. These cookies will bring the house down and demonstrate your vegan baking prowess for all to experience!

Courtesy of *Vegan Fusion World Cuisine*
Makes 12 large cookies

Dry Ingredients
2 cups spelt flour
1 cup vegan chocolate chips
1 cup walnuts – chopped
¾ cup rolled oats
½ teaspoon sea salt
¾ teaspoon baking soda
⅛ teaspoon cinnamon
1 pinch nutmeg

Wet Ingredients
⅔ cup maple syrup
⅔ cup safflower oil
2 tablespoon filtered water
1 teaspoon peppermint extract

1. Preheat oven to 350º. Place dry ingredients in a large mixing bowl and mix well. Combine wet ingredients in another large bowl. Add wet to dry and mix well.

2. Refrigerate for 15 minutes. Place 8 scoops on a well-oiled baking sheet and flatten slightly with hand. Space evenly so cookies have room to spread.

3. Bake until golden brown, approximately 10 minutes. Allow to cool before enjoying.

Variations

∾ For gluten-free, replace the spelt flour with 1 ¾ cups rice flour, ¼ cup sorghum, ¾ teaspoon xanthan gum. Add an additional 2 tablespoons of maple syrup.

∾ Replace the walnuts with toasted pecans or macadamia nuts.

∾ Replace the chocolate chips with carob chips or dried fruits.

∾ Add 2 tablespoon of cocoa or carob powder to above.

∾ Try adding 1 tablespoon spirulina.

Big Momma Freedom Chocolate Cake

Bring this cake to your next potluck and see who many people guess that its vegan. For an extra decadent experience, add 1 cup of chocolate chips to the wet ingredients. Have fun decorating the cake with coconut flakes, strawberries, colorful edible flowers, toasted pecans and/or chocolate chips.

Courtesy of *Vegan Fusion World Cuisine*
Makes one 9" x 13" cake

Dry Ingredients

2 ½ cups spelt flour

2 cups Sucanat

¾ cups cocoa Powder

1 ½ teaspoons baking soda

½ teaspoons sea salt, or to taste

½ teaspoons cinnamon powder

Wet Ingredients

6 tablespoons safflower oil

2 ¼ cups filtered water

2 tablespoons apple cider vinegar, raw

1 teaspoon vanilla extract

Frosting

2 cups chocolate chips

12.3 ounces silken firm tofu or ripe avocado

2 tablespoons maple syrup

1 ½ teaspoons vanilla extract, alcohol free

1. Cake: Preheat oven to 350°. Place dry ingredients in a large mixing bowl and mix well. Combine wet ingredients in a small bowl. Add wet to dry and mix well. Pour into a parchment paper lined 9" x 13" baking pan and bake until a toothpick comes out clean, approximately 35-40 minutes.

2. Frosting: Place chocolate chips in a double boiler on medium heat until chips are melted, stirring frequently. Combine with remaining ingredients and blend or food process until smooth and creamy. Refrigerate until it thickens.

3. Cool cake before frosting. Garnish with toasted coconut flakes, strawberries, edible flowers, toasted pecans and/or chocolate chips.

♥ Chocolate Mousse

Another essential dish in your French culinary repertoire, the chocolate mousse is a guaranteed crowd pleaser. A cooked and raw version of the dish is provided so you may compare the flavors and textures. The cooked version uses melted chocolate chips as well as coconut milk, while the raw version uses avocados and raw cacao powder to create the creamy base. Top with fresh berries and mint leaf for the perfect ending to any feast.

Courtesy of *The 30 Minute Vegan's Taste of Europe*

Cooked Version
Serves 4 to 6

1 ½ cups dark chocolate chips
½ cup plus 2 tablespoons coconut milk, regular or light variety
½ cup soy creamer or soy milk
2 tablespoons coconut oil, optional
3 tablespoons maple syrup, or to taste, depending on the sweetness of chips
2 teaspoons ground flax seeds mixed with 1 tablespoon water
½ teaspoon vanilla extract
⅛ teaspoon ground cinnamon
Pinch of cardamom and nutmeg
Pinch of sea salt
4 strawberries, sliced
8 mint leaves

1. Melt the chocolate chips in a double boiler. If you do not have a double boiler you can use any glass or steel bowl set on top of a pot with 1 to 2 inches of boiling water in it. Make sure that the bowl and anything you use to stir the chocolate with are completely dry. A good way to make sure the melting pot or bowl is dry is to start heating it before you put the chips in, this will dry

out any moisture. If water gets in contact with the chocolate it has the potential to become lumpy.

2. Pour into a small bowl and place in the freezer for 20 minutes or until just firm.

3. Transfer to a food processor or use a hand mixer and process until fluffy. Top with strawberries and mint leaves before serving.

♥ Raw Version
Serves 2 to 4

4 large medjool dates, pitted (¼ cup)
¼ cup water
1 large avocado, 1 cup mashed
3 tablespoons cacao powder
1 teaspoon ground flax seeds mixed with 1 tablespoon water
2 tablespoons coconut oil
Pinch of sea salt
Pinch of ground cinnamon, cardamom and nutmeg
½ teaspoon vanilla or seeds from 1 vanilla bean, optional
2 tablespoons agave nectar or maple syrup, or to taste
2 tablespoons dried coconut

1. Place the dates in a small bowl with ¼ cup water and allow to sit for 15 minutes.

2. Transfer the dates and date soak water to a food processor with all of the remaining ingredients except the coconut flakes, and process until smooth. Add more sweetener if necessary and process again.

3. Pour into individual serving bowls or one main serving dish and top with coconut flakes.

Variations
ᴄᴠ Add 1 teaspoon of different flavor extracts such as orange, hazelnut, coffee, or raspberry.

ᴄᴠ For a hint of heat, add ¼ teaspoon cayenne pepper or ½ teaspoon chili powder.

Raw Cheesecake

Extremely rich and satisfying, this recipe is for those special occasions when decadence is in order. To put it over the top, add a layer of Raw Chocolate Mousse (page 240) once the filling has a chance to set.

Courtesy of *Vegan Fusion Culinary Immersion*
Makes one 9-inch pie

Pie crust

1 ¼ cups pitted Medjool dates

1 ¼ cups almonds or filberts

2 tablespoon shredded coconut

¼ teaspoon cinnamon

Pinch of cardamom, nutmeg or allspice

Raw Cheese Filling

3 cups cashews – soaked for a minimum of 1hour

½ cup of lemon juice

½ teaspoon lemon zest

¾ cup agave nectar

2-4 tablespoons coconut oil (optional)

3 tablespoon nutritional yeast

1 teaspoon vanilla

1. Prepare the crust. Place the almonds or filberts in a food processor and process until just ground. Add dates, cinnamon, and cardamom and process until the dates are broken up and the mixture begins to run up the sides of the processor. You may need to add more dates if you are using a variety that is not as moist as the Medjool.

2. Use your hands to press the crust into a 9-inch pie pan. The crust should be approximately ¼ - ½ inch thick.

3. Prepare the filling by processing all of the ingredients in a food processor or a strong blender until completely creamy. Pour into the pie crust and place in the freezer until the filling solidifies, approximately 2 hours. Transfer to the refrigerator for an hour before slicing. Top with fresh berries, sliced fruit designs, edible flowers, and or shredded coconut.

Variations

ༀ Add ¾ cup seed or nut milk and 3 tablespoons of lecithin to filling before processing.

ༀ Top with a layer of chocolate mousse!

ༀ Create different crusts by adding ¼ cup raw cacao and/or 2 tablespoons of nut butter. Replace almonds with other nuts. Replace dates with figs, apricots or other dried fruits.

ༀ Crust can also be used to create bliss balls – add seeds, raw cacao nibs, spirulina or other superfoods. Roll in dried coconut or raw cacao powder.

ABOUT THE AUTHORS

Sarah Taylor, MBA

Sarah Taylor became a vegan in 2002 after reading *Diet for a New America* by John Robbins. At the time, the vegan diet was relatively unknown, so in 2006, Sarah started a company called "The Vegan Next Door," (www.TheVeganNextDoor.com) with a mission of teaching people about the vegan diet.

In 2008, Sarah's first vegan book, *Vegan in 30 Days*, was released, and has since sold thousands of copies in multiple languages. In 2010, Sarah completed her Certificate in Plant Based Nutrition from Cornell University. She worked as a Motivational Speaker for Joel Fuhrman, MD, author of *Eat to Live,* and is on faculty at the Nutritional Education Institute. Sarah has been interviewed for countless TV, radio and internet shows, including NPR, PBS and EarthSave Radio, among others. She is an author for VegNews magazine, an expert blogger at www.VegSource.com and also runs her own blog at www.blogspot. thevegannextdoor.com.

In her personal time, Sarah enjoys playing tennis, scuba diving, studying spirituality and adventure traveling. She is also the inventor of The Stackable Gourmet (www.StackableGourmet. com), an innovative kitchen tool first launched on the Home Shopping Network that creates attractive and gourmet stacked food. She is happily married and lives in Gig Harbor, WA with her husband and many pets.

Mark Reinfeld

Mark Reinfeld is the winner of Vegan.com's Recipe of the Year Award for 2011 and has over 20 years experience preparing creative vegan and raw food cuisine. Mark is described by VegCooking.com as being "poised on the leading edge of contemporary vegan cooking." He is the founding chef of the Blossoming Lotus Restaurant, winner of Honolulu Advertiser's 'Ilima Award for "Best Restaurant on Kaua'i." Mark is also the recipient of a Platinum Carrot Award for living foods – a national award given by the Aspen Center of Integral Health to America's top "innovative and trailblazing healthy chefs."

Mark received his initial culinary training from his grandfather Ben Bimstein, a renowned chef and ice carver in New York City. He developed his love for World culture and cuisine during travel journeys through Europe, Asia and the Middle East. In 1997, Mark formed the Blossoming Lotus Personal Chef Service in Malibu, California. To further his knowledge of the healing properties of food, he received a Masters Degree in Holistic Nutrition.

His first cookbook, Vegan World Fusion Cuisine, coauthored with Bo Rinaldi and with a foreword by Dr. Jane Goodall, has won several national awards, including "Cookbook of the Year," "Best New Cookbook," "Best Book by a Small Press" and a Gourmand Award for "Best Vegetarian Cookbook in the USA." In addition, Mark authored *The 30 Minute Vegan's Taste of Europe* and coauthored *The 30 Minute Vegan's Taste of the East*, *The 30 Minute Vegan* and *The Complete Idiot's Guide to Eating Raw.*

Mark currently offers an online vegan culinary course at www. CookingHealthyLessons.comas well as vegan cooking and raw food preparation consulting, workshops, chef training, immersions and vegan culinary retreats world-wide.

Special Thanks to Laurelee Blanchard

In 1997, Laurelee Blanchard left a lucrative career in commercial real estate to work full time raising awareness about the plight of animals raised for food on factory farms. She served as Director of Communication for Farm Animal Rights Movement (FARM), as a campaign consultant to Farm Sanctuary, Director of the Vegetarian Society of Hawaii, and consultant to the World Society for the Protection of Animals. She won a "Vegan of the Year" award in 2011 for convincing several supermarket chains to stop buying pork from pigs transported alive from the mainland U.S. to Hawaii, thereby ending the long-distance ocean transport of 6,000 pigs a year to Hawaii for slaughter, and likely resulting in the closure of the State's largest slaughterhouse.

Laurelee founded Leilani Farm Sanctuary on Maui with the mission of providing care for rescued animals and educating the community about factory farming and the importance of plant-based eating. The sanctuary conducts tours for local residents and vacationers from all over the world, offering visitors a unique opportunity to interact closely with animals commonly regarded as food, and experience them as individuals with endearing personalities. Visitors to the sanctuary receive vegan starter guides and regular ongoing newsletters that contain factual information and vegan recipes to help them continue on a vegan path. You can learn more about Laurelee and Leilani Farm Sanctuary at www.Leilani FarmSanctuary.org.

REFERENCES

1   Blayney D.P. *The Changing Landscape of U.S. Milk Production.* United States Dept. of Agriculture, Statistical Bulletin #978, June 2002.

2   Dasa, S. *Cows are Cool.* Soul Science University Press, 2009. Pg 9.

3   Purdue News, December 2000. http://www.purdue.edu/uns/html4ever/0012.Pajor.well.html. Retrieved 5 Oct 2012.

4   Waynert DF et al., *The Response of Beef Cattle to Noise During Handling.* Applied Animal Behaviour Science 62:1 (1999): 27-42.

5   McDonald, J. M., et al., *Changes in the Size and Location of U.S. Dairy Farms,* Profits, Costs and the Changing Structure of Dairy Farming, ERR-47 Sept. 2007.

6   http://abcnews.go.com/Blotter/dehorning-standard-practice-dairy-farms/story?id=9658414#.T7MkDs2xD9A

7   Gulliksen, S.M., et al (2009) *Calf mortality in Norwegian dairy herds.* J Dairy Sci, 92, 2782-2795.

8   Faubert, G.M. & Litvinsky, Y. (2000) *Natural transmission of Cryptosporidium parvum between dams and calves on a dairy farm.* J Parasitol, 86, 495-500.

9   Gulliksen, S.M., et al. (2009) *Calf mortality in Norwegian dairy herds.* J Dairy Sci, 92, 2782-2795.

10 Dasa, S. *Cows are Cool.* Soul Science University Press, 2009. Pg 38.

11 Dasa, S. *Cows are Cool.* Soul Science University Press, 2009. Pg 39.

12 Levy, F., K. M. Kendrick, J. A. Goode, R. Guevara-Guzman and E. B. Keverne. 1995. *Oxytocin and vasopressin release in the olfactory bulb of parturient ewes: Changes with maternal experience and effects on acetylcholine, gamma-aminobutyric acid, glutamate and noradrenaline release.* Brain Res. 669(2):197-206.

13 Flower FC, Weary DM – Institute of Ecology and Resource Management, School of Agriculture, Edinburgh, UK. *Effects of early separation on the dairy cow and calf: 2. Separation at 1 day and 2 weeks after birth.* Retrieved 2009-05-29.

14 http://www.milkingmanagement.co.uk/contents/Why%20Mastitis.htm

15 American Dairy Science Association, 2001.

16 *SCC, BC Counts & Antibiotic Residue Violations* – J Dairy Sci. 2002 April 85(4):782-789.

17 Veterinary Medicine (5th ed.), London: Baillière Tindall, 1979, pp. 827–836 (Parturient paresis or milk fever), ISBN 0-7020-07-18-8

18 *Report of the Scientific Veterinary Committee Subgroup – Bovine Immunodeficiency Virus.* June 1996. http://ec.europa.eu/food/fs/sc/oldcomm4/out32_en.pdf. Retrieved May 2012.

19 Gonda, Matthew A. *Bovine Immunodeficiency Virus.* AIDS. 1992. pp. 759–776.

20 *Bovine Leukemia.* http://www.vetmed.ucdavis.edu/vetext/INF-DA/INF-DA_BovineLeukemia.html

21 *Bovine Leukosis Virus on U.S. Dairy Operations,* 2007 (PDF). NAHMS Dairy 2007. U.S. Department of Agriculture.

22 *Bovine Leukemia.* http://www.vetmed.ucdavis.edu/vetext/INF-DA/INF-DA_BovineLeukemia.html

23 *Paratuberculosis.* Merck Veterinary Manual, 8th ed. Edited by S.E. Aiello. Whitehouse Station, NJ: Merck and Co. 1998.

24 Faubert, G.M. & Litvinsky, Y. (2000) *Natural transmission of Cryptosporidium parvum between dams and calves on a dairy farm.* J Parasitol, 86, 495-500. Johnson-Ifearulundu Y, Kaneene JB. *Distribution and environmental risk factors for paratuberculosis in dairy cattle herds in Michigan.* Am J Vet Res. 1999 May;60(5):589-96.

25 Prusiner SB. *Prions.* (November 1998) Proceedings of the National Academy of Sciences of the United States of America 95 (23): 13363–83. doi:10.1073/pnas.95.23.13363. PMC 33918. PMID 9811807. Retrieved 2010-02-28.

26 *BSE Inquiry, Statement No. 476.* BSE Inquiry. 1999-05-07. Statement of David Osborne Hagger, Head of Abridged Licensing and Coordinator of the Executive support business of the Medicines Division of the Department of Health at Market Towers in London. Retrieved 5 Oct 2012.

27 Manspeaker JE. *Metritis and Endometritis.* Dairy Integrated Reproductive Management. IRM-22.

28 Gilbert RO, et al. *Prevalence of endometritis and its effects on reproductive performance of dairy cows.* Theriogenology 64 (2005) 1879–1888.

29 Guard, C. *Recognizing and managing infectious causes of lameness in cattle.* The AABP Proceedings, January 1995, No. 27, p. 80-82.

30 Grandin, Temple: Johnson, Catherine (2009). *Animals Make Us Human.* New York, NY: Houghton, Mifflin, Harcourt Publishing Company. pg. 164.

31 Shearer JK, Van Amstel S. *Lameness in Dairy Cattle. Proceedings from the 2000 Kentucky Dairy Conference.* http://www.healthyhooves.com/pdffiles/dr%20shearer.pdf. Retrived May 25, 2012.

32 http://www.merckvetmanual.com/mvm/index.jsp?cfile=htm/bc/90526.htm. Retrieved May 17, 2012.

33 Shearer JK, Van Amstel S. *Lameness in Dairy Cattle.* Proceedings from the 2000 Kentucky Dairy Conference. http://www.healthyhooves.com/pdffiles/dr%20shearer.pdf. Retrived May 25, 2012.

34 Philipot JM, et al. *Risk factors of dairy cow lameness associated with housing conditions.* Vet Res. 1994;25(2-3):244-8.

35 Wallace, Richard L. *Market Cows: A Potential Profit Center.* University of Illinois Extension. 13 Mar 2002.

36 Wallace, Richard L. *Market Cows: A Potential Profit Center.* University of Illinois Extension. 13 Mar 2002.

37 Wallace, Richard L. *Market Cows: A Potential Profit Center.* University of Illinois Extension. 13 Mar 2002.

38 Economics Research Service, *U.S. Beef and Cattle Industry: Background Statistics and Information,* USDA 10 July 2010.

39 Warrick J. The Washington Post. April 10, 2001. Front Page.

40 Economics Research Service, *U.S. Beef and Cattle Industry: Background Statistics and Information,* USDA 25 May 2011.

41 *Compassion in World Farming – Poultry.* Ciwf.org.uk. Retrieved 2012-01-12.

42 *Compassion in World Farming – Egg laying hens.* Ciwf.org.uk. Retrieved 2012-01-12.

43 North, Mack O.; Donald E. Bell (1990). *Commercial Chicken Production Manual* (4th ed.). Van Nostrand Reinhold. pp. 297, 315.

44 http://www.uepcertified.com/program/guidelines/categories/housing-space-feed-water. United Egg Producers.

45 Appleby, M.C.; J.A. Mench and B.O. Hughes (2004). *Poultry Behaviour and Welfare.* Wallingford and Cambridge MA: CABI Publishing.

46 *Welfare Issues with Laying Hens.* http://www.ciwf.org.uk/farm_animals/poultry/egg_laying_hens/welfare_issues.aspx Retrieved 2012-01-12.

47 *National Broiler Chicken Microbiological Baseline Data Collection Program.* USDA. http://www.fsis.usda.gov/OPHS/baseline/broiler1.pdf Retrieved 2012-01-13.

References

[48] Scientific Veterinary Committee of the European Commission (1996). *Report on the Welfare of Layer Hen.*

[49] Sherwin, C.M., Richards, G.J and Nicol, C.J. 2010. *Comparison of the welfare of layer hens in 4 housing systems in the UK.* British Poultry Science, 51(4): 488-499.

[50] Gregory NG and Wilkins LJ, *Broken Bones in Domestic Fowl: Handling and Processing Damage in End-of-Lay Battery Hens*, British Poultry Science 30:3 (1989): 555-562.

[51] Huber-Eicher, B. and Sebo, F. 2001. *The prevalence of feather pecking and development in commercial flocks of laying hens.* Applied Animal Behaviour Science, 74: 223–231.

[52] Rodenburg, B.T., Komen, H., Ellen, E.D., Uitdehaag, K.A. and van Arendonk, J.A., 2008. *Selection method and early-life history affect behavioural development, feather pecking and cannibalism in laying hens: A review.* Applied Animal Behaviour Science 110: 217–228.

[53] Keeling, L.J., Hughes, B.O. and Dun, P., (1988). *Performance of free range laying hens in a polythene house and their behaviour on range.* Farm Building Progress, 94: 21-28.

[54] Sherwin, C.M., Richards. G.J. and Nicol, C.J., (2010). *Comparison of the welfare of layer hens in 4 housing systems in the UK.* British Poultry Science, 51: 488-499.

[55] Weitzenburger, D., Vits, A., Hamann, H. and Distl, O., (2005). *Effect of furnished small group housing systems and furnished cages on mortality and causes of death in two layer strains.* British Poultry Science, 46: 553-559.

[56] Krause E.T., Petow, S. and Kjaer J.B. (2011). *A note on the physiological and behavioural consequences of cannibalistic toe pecking in laying hens (Gallus gallus domesticus).* Archiv Fur Geflugelkunde, 75: 140-143.

[57] Olsson, I.A.S. and Keeling, L.J., 2005. *Why in earth? Dustbathing behaviour in jungle and domestic fowl reviewed from a Tinbergian and animal welfare perspective.* Applied Animal Behaviour Science, 93: 259-282.

[58] Lindberg, A.C. and Nicol, C.J. 1997. *Dustbathing in modified battery cages: is sham dustbathing an adequate substitute?* Applied Animal Behaviour Science, 55: 113–128.

[59] Grandin, Temple: Johnson, Catherine (2009). *Animals Make Us Human.* New York, NY: Houghton, Mifflin, Harcourt Publishing Company. pg. 15.

[60] Rushen J and Mason G, *A Decade-or-More's Progress in Understanding Stereotypic Behavior.* Stereotypic Animal Behaviour, ed. Rushen & Mason, pg. 196.

[61] Ralph, C.L. 1960. *Polydipsia in the hen following lesions in the supraoptic hypothalamus.* American Journal of Physiology, 198:528-530.

[62] Lay Jr., D.C., Fulton, R.M., Hester, P.Y., Karcher, D.M., Kjaer, J.B., Mench, J.A., Mullens, B.A., Newberry, R.C., C.J., O'Sullivan, N.P. and Porter, R.E., (2011). *Hen welfare in different housing systems.* Poultry Science, 90: 278-294.

[63] Grandin, Temple: Johnson, Catherine (2005). *Animals in Translation.* New York, NY: Scribner. p. 183.

[64] Singer, Peter (2006). *In Defense of Animals.* Wiley-Blackwell. p. 176.

[65] Chen, B.L., Haith, K.L. and Mullens, B.A., (2011). *Beak condition drives abundance and grooming-mediated competitive asymmetry in a poultry ectoparasite community.* Parasitology, 138: 748-757.

[66] Breward, J. and Gentle, M.J. 1985. *Neuroma formation and abnormal afferent nerve discharges after partial beak amputation (beak trimming) in poultry.* Experientia, 41: 1132-1134.

[67] Falkenberg, G., Fleissner, G., Schuchardt, K., Kuehbacher, M., Thalau, P., Mouritsen, H., Heyers, D., Wellenreuther, G. and Fleissner. G., (2010). *Avian magnetoreception: Elaborate iron mineral containing dendrites in the upper beak seem to be a common feature of birds.* PLoS ONE 5:e9231.

[68] Wiltschko, W., Freire, R., Munro, U., Ritz, T., Rogers, L.J., Thalau,P., and Wiltschko. R., (2007). *The magnetic compass of domestic chicken*, Gallus gallus. Journal Experimental Biology, 210:2300–2310.

[69] Freire, R., Eastwood, M.A. and Joyce, M., (2011). *Minor beak trimming in chickens leads to loss of mechanoreception and magnetoreception.* Journal of Animal Science, 89:1201–1206.

[70] Lay Jr., D.C., Fulton, R.M., Hester, P.Y., Karcher, D.M., Kjaer, J.B., Mench, J.A., Mullens, B.A., Newberry, R.C., C.J., O'Sullivan, N.P. and Porter, R.E., (2011). *Hen welfare in different housing systems.* Poultry Science, 90: 278-294.

[71] Green, L.E., Lewis, K., Kimpton, A. and Nicol, C.J., 2000. *Cross-sectional study of the prevalence of feather pecking in laying hens in alternative systems and its association with management and disease.* Veterinary Record, 147: 233-238.

[72] Harrison, P.C., Bercovitz, A.B. and Leary, G.A. 1968. *Development of eye enlargement of domestic fowl subjected to low light intensity.* International Journal of Biometeorology, 12: 351-358.

[73] Siopes, T.D., Timmons, M.B., Baughman, G.R., Parkhurst, C.R. 1984. *The effects of light intensity on turkey poult performance, eye morphology and adrenal weight.* Poultry Science, 63: 904-909.

[74] Prescott, N.B. and Wathes, C.M. 2002. *Preference and motivation of laying hens to eat under different illuminances and the effect of illuminance on eating behaviour.* British Poultry Science, 43: 190-195.

[75] Davis, N.J., Prescott, N.B., Savory, C.J. and Wathes, C.M. 1999. *Preferences of growing fowls for different light intensities in relation to age, strain and behaviour.* Animal Welfare, 8: 193-203.

[76] Gunnarsson, S., Keeling, L.J. and Svedberg, J., (1999). *Effects of rearing factors on the prevalence of floor eggs, cloacal cannibalism and feather pecking in commercial flocks of loose housed laying hens.* British Poultry Science, 40: 12–18.

[77] Cordiner LS and Savory CJ, *Use of Perches and Nestboxes by Laying Hens in Relation to Social Status, Based on Examination of Consistency of Rankimg Orders and Frequency of Interaction,* Applied Animal Behaviour Science 71:4 (2001): 305-317.

[78] Webster, A.B., (2003). *Physiology and behavior of the hen during induced moult.* Poultry Science, 82: 992-1002.

[79] North, Mack O. and Bell, Donald D, *Commercial Chicken Production Manual*, 4th ed., 1990. Van Nostrand Reinhold, pp. 438.

[80] Yousaf, M. and Chaudhry, A.S., (2008). *History, changing scenarios and future strategies to induce moulting in laying hens.* World's Poultry Science Journal, 64: 65-75.

[81] Lambton, S.L., Knowles, T.G., Yorke, C. and Nicol, C.J., 2010. *The risk factors affecting the development of gentle and severe feather pecking in loose housed laying hens.* Applied Animal Behaviour Science 123: 32–42.

[82] Green, L.E., Lewis, K., Kimpton, A. and Nicol, C.J., 2000. *Cross-sectional study of the prevalence of feather pecking in laying hens in alternative systems and its association with management and disease.* Veterinary Record, 147: 233-238.

[83] Bestman, M.W.P. and Wagenaar, J.P. 2003. *Farm level factors associated with feather pecking in organic laying hens.* Livestock Production Science, 80: 133–140.

[84] Morris, M.C. (2006). *The Ethics and Politics of the Caged Layer Hen Debate in New Zealand.* Journal of Agricultural and Environmental Ethics 19: 495–514.

[85] USCA Chapter 48 Section 1902. http://www.gpo.gov/fdsys/pkg/USCODE-2011-title7/pdf/USCODE-2011-title7-chap48.pdf Retrieved 22 Oct 2012.

[86] *Is Honey Vegan?* http://www.compassionatespirit.com/is-honey-vegan.htm Retrieved February 2012.

[87] USDA Nutrient Data Laboratory. *Honey.* Retrieved 24 August 2007.

[88] Martos I, Ferreres F, Tomás-Barberán F (2000). *Identification of flavonoid markers for the botanical origin of Eucalyptus honey.* J Agric Food Chem 48 (5): 1498–502.

[89] Campbell TC, Campbell TM. *The China Study*, Dallas, TX: Benbella Books, 2004.

[90] Madhavan TV, and Gopalan C. *The effect of dietary protein on carcinogenesis of aflatoxin.* Arch. Path. 85 (1968):133-137.

[91] Madhavan TV, and Gopalan C. *The effect of dietary protein on carcinogenesis of aflatoxin.* Arch. Path. 85 (1968):133-137.

[92] Carroll KK. *Experimental Evidence of dietary factors and hormone-dependent cancers.* Cancer Res 1975;35:3374-3383.

[93] Ganmaa D and Sato A, *The possible role of female sex hormones in milk from pregnant cows in the development of breast, ovarian and corpus uteri cancers.* Med Hypotheses. 2005;65(6):1028-37. Epub 2005 Aug 24.

[94] Ganmaa D and Sato A, *The possible role of female sex hormones in milk from pregnant cows in the development of breast, ovarian and corpus uteri cancers.* Med Hypotheses. 2005;65(6):1028-37.

[95] Ganmaa D and Sato A, *The possible role of female sex hormones in milk from pregnant cows in the development of breast, ovarian and corpus uteri cancers.* Med Hypotheses. 2005;65(6):1028-37. Epub 2005 Aug 24.

[96] Ganmaa D and Sato A, *The possible role of female sex hormones in milk from pregnant cows in the development of breast, ovarian and corpus uteri cancers.* Med Hypotheses. 2005;65(6):1028-37. Epub 2005 Aug 24.

[97] Arnaldez FI, et al. *Targeting the insulin growth factor receptor 1.* Hematol Oncol Clin North Am. 2012 Jun 26;(3)527-42, vii-viii. Epub 2012 Feb 28.

[98] Miura, Y.; Kato, H.; Noguchi, T. (2007). *Effect of dietary proteins on insulin-like growth factor-1 (IGF-1) messenger ribonucleic acid content in rat liver.* British Journal of Nutrition 67 (2): 257.

[99] Hankinson SE, Willett WC, et al. *Circulating concentrations of insulin-like growth factor I and risk of breast cancer.* Lancet, Volume 351, Issue 9113, Pages 1393 - 1396, 9 May 1998

[100] Chan JM, Stampfer MJ, et al. *Plasma insulin-like growth factor-I and prostate cancer risk: a prospective study.* Science. 1998 Jan 23;279(5350):563-6.

[101] Kaaks, R. Toniolo P, et al. *Serum C-peptide, insulin-like growth factor (IGF)-I, IGF-binding proteins, and colorectal cancer risk in women.* J Natl Cancer Inst. 2000 Oct 4;92(19):1592-600.

[102] Kushi LH, Mink PJ, Folsom AR, et al. *Prospective study of diet and ovarian cancer.* Am J Epidemiol. 1999;149:21–31.

[103] Giovannucci E, Rimm EB, Wolk A, et al. *Calcium and fructose intake in relation to risk of prostate cancer.* Cancer Res. 1998; 58:442–447.

[104] Chan JM, Stampfer MJ, et al. *Dairy products, calcium, and prostate cancer risk in the Physicians' Health Study.* Am J Clin Nutr. 2001 Oct;74(4):549-54.

[105] Heaney RP, McCarron DA, et al. *Dietary changes favorably affect bone remodeling in older adults.* J Am Diet Assoc1999;99:1228–33.

[106] Oliver MF. *Diet and Coronary Heart Disease.* Hum Nutr Clin Nutr. 1982;36(6):413-27.

[107] USDA, *Dietary Guidelines for Americans*, 2010. Jan 2011. Pg 26.

[108] USDA, *Dietary Guidelines for Americans*, 2010. Jan 2011. Pg 24.

[109] Howard BV, et al. *Low-fat dietary pattern and risk of cardiovascular disease: the Women's Health Initiative Randomized Controlled Dietary Modification Trial.* JAMA. 2006 Feb 8;295(6):655-66.

[110] de Lorgeril, et al. *Mediterranean Diet, Traditional Risk Factors, and the Rate of Cardiovascular Complications After Myocardial Infarction; Final Report of the Lyon diet Heart Study.* Circulation, 1999 Feb 16;99(6):779-85.

[111] Esselstyn CB Jr. *Updating a 12-year experience with arrest and reversal therapy for coronary heart disease (an overdue requiem for palliative cardiology).* Am J Cardiology. 1999 Aug, 84(3):Pages 339-341.

[112] Vogel RA. *Brachial artery ultrasound: a noninvasive tool in the assessment of triglyceride-rich lipoproteins.* Clin Cardiol. 1999 Jun;22(6 Suppl):II34-9.

[113] Vogel RA, Corretti MC, Plotnick GD. *The postprandial effect of components of the Mediterranean diet on endothelial function.* J of Amer Col Card. 2000 Nov;36(5).

[114] Djousse L, Gaziano JM. *Egg consumption in relation to cardiovascular disease and mortality: the Physicians' Health Study.* Am J Clin Nutr 2008;87:964-969.

[115] Weggemans RM, Zock PL, Katan MB. *Dietary cholesterol from eggs increases the ratio of total cholesterol to high-density lipoprotein cholesterol in humans: a meta-analysis.* Am J Clin Nutr 2001;73:885-891.

[116] Li Y, Zhou C, Zhou S, LiL. Egg consumption and risk of cardiovascular diseases and eiabetes: A meta-analysis. *Atherosclerosis.* Published ahead of print April 17, 2013.

[117] Physician's Committee for Responsible Medicine. *Good Medicine.* Autumn 2012: Vol XXI, No. 4. Pg 7.

[118] Hannan EL, Magaziner J, Wang JJ, et al. (2001). *Mortality and locomotion 6 months after hospitalization for hip fracture: risk factors and risk-adjusted hospital outcomes.* JAMA 285 (21): 2736–42.

[119] *Osteoporosis: fast facts.* National Osteoporosis Foundation. Accessed January 24, 2008.

[120] Food and Agriculture Organization of the United Nations. *FAO Production Yearbook.* Rome, 1987. Grams/caput/day 1983-85. p 247.

[121] Cummings SR, Kelsey, JL, et al. *Epidemiology of osteoporosis and osteoporotic fractures.* Epidemiol. Rev. 1985;7:178-208.

[122] Hegsted DM. *Calcium and Osteoporosis.* J. Nutr. 116 (1986):2316-2319.

[123] Feskanich D, Willett WC, Stampfer MJ, Colditz GA. *Milk, dietary calcium, and bone fractures in women: a 12-year prospective study.* Am J Publ Health 1997;87:992-7.

[124] Cumming RG, Klineberg RJ. *Case-control study of risk factors for hip fractures in the elderly.* Am J Epidemiol 1994;139:493-503.

[125] Sellmeyer DE, Stone KL, Sebastian A, et al. *A high ratio of dietary animal to vegetable protein increases the rate of bone loss and the risk of fracture in postmenopausal women.* Am. J. Clin. Nutr. 73(2001):118-122.

[126] Owusu W, Willett WC, Feskanich D, Ascherio A, Spiegelman D, Colditz GA. *Calcium intake and the incidence of forearm and hip fractures among men.* J Nutr. 1997; 127:1782–87.

[127] Feskanich D, Willett WC, Stampfer MJ, Colditz GA. *Milk, dietary calcium, and bone fractures in women: a 12-year prospective study.* Am J Public Health. 1997; 87:992–97.

[128] Swank, RI. *Effect of low saturated fat diet in early and late cases of multiple sclerosis.* Lancet 336[1990]:37-39.

[129] Ghadirian P, Jain M, et al. *Nutritional factors in the aetiology of multiple sclerosis: a case-control study in Montreal, Canada.* Int J Epidemiol. 1998 Oct;27(5):845-852.

References

[130] Malosse D, Perron H, Sasco A, et al. *Correlation between milk and dairy product consumption and multiple sclerosis prevalence: a worldwide study.* Neuroepidemiology 11 (1992): 304-312.

[131] Trichopoulou A, Psaltopoulou T, Orfanos P, et al. *Diet and physical activity in relation to overall mortality amongst adult diabetics in a general population cohort.* J Intern Med 2006;259:583-591.

[132] Li Y, Zhou C, Zhou S, LiL. Egg consumption and risk of cardiovascular diseases and eiabetes: A meta-analysis. *Atherosclerosis.* Published ahead of print April 17, 2013.

[133] Barnard ND, Cohen J, et al. *A low-fat vegan diet improves glycemic control and cardiovascular risk factors in a randomized clinical trial in individuals with type 2 diabetes.* Diabetes Care. 2006 Aug;29(8):1777-83.

[134] Hu FB, van Dam RM, Liu S. *Diet and Risk of Type II Diabetes: The role of types of fat and carbohydrates.* Diabetologia (2001) 44: 805-817.

[135] Knip M, Virtanen SM, et al. *Early feeding and risk of type 1 diabetes: experiences from the Trial to Reduce Insulin-dependent diabetes mellitus in the Genetically at Risk (TRIGR).* Am J Clin Nutr. 2011 Dec;94(6 Suppl):1814S-1820S.

[136] Anderson JW. *Dietary fiber in nutrition management of diabetes.* In: G. Vahouny, V and D. Kritchevsky (eds.), Dietary Fiber: Basic and Clinical Aspects, pp343-360. New York: Plenum Press, 1986.

[137] emedicine.medscape.com/article/187249-overview

[138] Kneepkens CM, Meijer Y. *Clinical practice. Diagnosis and treatment of cow's milk allergy.* Eur J Pediatr 2009 Aug, 168(8):891-896.

[139] Panksepp J, Narmansell L, Siviy S, Rossi J, Zolovick AJ. *Casomorphins reduce separation distress in chicks.* Peptides 1984;5:829-31.

[140] Azzouz A, et al. *Simultaneous Determination of 20 Pharmacologically Active Substances in Cow's Milk, Goat's Milk, and Human Breast Milk by Gas Chromatography – Mass Spectrometry.* J. Agric. Food Chem., 2011, 59 (9), pp 5125–5132.

[141] Keon J. *Whitewash.* British Columbia, Canada, New Society Publishers. 2010. Pgs 89-91.

[142] Keon J. *Whitewash.* British Columbia, Canada, New Society Publishers. 2010. Pgs 89-91.

[143] United Nations Food and Agriculture Organization. *Livestock's Long Shadow. Environmental Issues and Options.* 2006 Pg xx.

[144] Meehl et al., *Chap. 10: Global Climate Projections, Sec. 10.ES: Mean Temperature,* in IPCC AR4 WG1 2007.

[145] Robbins, J. *The Food Revolution.* San Francisco, CA. Conari Press 2001, Pg 263.

[146] United Nations Food and Agriculture Organization. *Livestock's Long Shadow. Environmental Issues and Options.* 2006, Pg 80.

[147] United Nations Food and Agriculture Organization. *Livestock's Long Shadow. Environmental Issues and Options.* 2006, Pg 5.

[148] Lobell, David; Burke, Tebaldi, Mastrandrea, Falcon, Naylor (2008). *Prioritizing climate change adaptation needs for food security in 2030.* Science 319 (5863): 607–10. DOI:10.1126/science.1152339. PMID 18239122. Retrieved April 2012.

[149] Kiehl, J.T.; Trenberth, K.E. (1997). *Earth's Annual Global Mean Energy Budget.* Bulletin of the American Meteorological Society 78 (2): 197–208. Archived from the original on 24 June 2008. Retrieved 21 April 2009.

[150] Schmidt, Gavin (6 April 2005). *Water vapour: feedback or forcing?* RealClimate. Retrieved 21 April 2009.

[151] Russell, Randy (16 May 2007). *The Greenhouse Effect & Greenhouse Gases.* University Corporation for Atmospheric Research Windows to the Universe. Retrieved 27 December 2009.

[152] *America's Climate Choices.* Washington, D.C.: The National Academies Press. 2011. p. 15. ISBN 978-0-309-14585-5.

[153] Meehl et al., *Chap. 10: Global Climate Projections,* Sec. 10.ES: Mean Temperature, in IPCC AR4 WG1 2007.

[154] *Climate Change 2001: Working Group I: The Scientific Basis: figure 6-6.* Retrieved 1 May 2006.

[155] Ciborowski, P. *Sources, Sinks, Trends and Opportunities,* in Abrahamson D., ed., The Challenge of Global Warming (Island Press, 1989.)

[156] United Nations Food and Agriculture Organization. *Livestock's Long Shadow. Environmental Issues and Options.* 2006, Pg xxi

[157] United Nations Food and Agriculture Organization. *Livestock's Long Shadow. Environmental Issues and Options.* 2006, Pg 90.

[158] *Food Consumption and Its Environmental Impact.* Sierra Club. http://www.sierraclub.org/sustainable_consumption/food_factsheet.asp. Retrieved June 7, 2012.

[159] United Nations Food and Agriculture Organization. *Livestock's Long Shadow. Environmental Issues and Options.* 2006, Pg xxi

[160] United Nations Food and Agriculture Organization. *Livestock's Long Shadow. Environmental Issues and Options.* 2006, Pg xxi.

[161] United Nations Food and Agriculture Organization. *Livestock's Long Shadow. Environmental Issues and Options.* 2006, Pg 86.

[162] United Nations Food and Agriculture Organization. *Livestock's Long Shadow. Environmental Issues and Options.* 2006, Pg 88.

[163] United Nations Food and Agriculture Organization. *Livestock's Long Shadow. Environmental Issues and Options.* 2006, Pg 89.

[164] United Nations Food and Agriculture Organization. *Livestock's Long Shadow. Environmental Issues and Options.* 2006, Pg 100.

[165] Capper JL, Cady RA, Buman DE. *The Environmental Impact of Dairy Production: 1944 Compared with 2007.* Journal of Animal Science, March 13, 2009. Pg 230.

[166] Ciborowski, P. *Sources, Sinks, Trends and Opportunities,* in Abrahamson D., ed., The Challenge of Global Warming (Island Press, 1989.)

[167] Halweil, B. *United States Leads World Meat Stampede,* Worldwatch Issues Paper, July 2, 1998.

[168] www.epa.gov/climatechange/emissions/usinventoryreport.html. Retrieved June 2012.

[169] United Nations Food and Agriculture Organization. *Livestock's Long Shadow. Environmental Issues and Options.* 2006, Pg 114.

[170] EPA (2007). *Recent Climate Change: Atmosphere Changes.* Climate Change Science Program. United States Environmental Protection Agency. Retrieved 21 April 2009.

[171] IPCC, *Summary for Policymakers, Concentrations of atmospheric greenhouse gases,* p. 7, in IPCC TAR WG1 2001.

[172] Steinfeld et al., 2006

[173] United Nations Food and Agriculture Organization. *Livestock's Long Shadow. Environmental Issues and Options.* 2006, Pg 112.

[174] Bittman, M. *We Could Be Heroes,* New York Times, May 15, 2012.

[175] United Nations Food and Agriculture Organization. *Livestock's Long Shadow. Environmental Issues and Options.* 2006, Pg 83.

[176] Ebert, T. *The Dangerous Truth: Why Eating Meat is Ruining Your Health and Destroying the Environment.* Pg. 18-19.

[177] http://www.cdc.gov/asthma/asthmadata.htm. Retrieved 3 Aug 2012.

[178] Woolf, Jim. *Have Hogs Caused Milford Maladies?* Salt Lake Tribune, January 26, 2000.

[179] United Nations Food and Agriculture Organization. *Livestock's Long Shadow. Environmental Issues and Options.* 2006, Pg 114.

[180] United Nations Food and Agriculture Organization. *Livestock's Long Shadow. Environmental Issues and Options.* 2006, Pg 125.

[181] United Nations Food and Agriculture Organization. *Livestock's Long Shadow. Environmental Issues and Options.* 2006, Pg 126.

[182] Dennehy, K.F. (2000). *High Plains regional ground-water study: U.S. Geological Survey Fact Sheet FS-091-00.* USGS. Retrieved 2012-06-21.

[183] Larsen J. *Meat Consumption in China Now Double That in the U.S.* Earth Policy Institute Plan B Updates. http://www.earth-policy.org/plan_b_updates/2012/update102. Retrieved June 7, 2012.

[184] United Nations Food and Agriculture Organization. *Livestock's Long Shadow. Environmental Issues and Options.* 2006, Pg 126.

[185] United Nations Food and Agriculture Organization. *Livestock's Long Shadow. Environmental Issues and Options.* 2006, Pg 133.

[186] Ayres, E. *Will We Still Eat Meat?* Time Magazine, Nov 8, 1999. Vol 154 Issue 19 pg 107.

[187] World Business Counsel for Sustainable Development. *WBCSD Water Facts & Trends.* Retrieved 2009-03-12.

[188] United Nations Food and Agriculture Organization. *Livestock's Long Shadow. Environmental Issues and Options.* 2006, Pg 126.

[189] United Nations Food and Agriculture Organization. *Livestock's Long Shadow. Environmental Issues and Options.* 2006, Pg 130.

[190] United Nations Food and Agriculture Organization. *Livestock's Long Shadow. Environmental Issues and Options.* 2006, Pg 129.

[191] Ayres, E. *Will We Still Eat Meat?* Time Magazine, Nov 8, 1999. Vol 154 Issue 19 pg 107.

[192] Robbins, J. *The Food Revolution.* San Francisco, CA. Conari Press 2001. Pg 292.

[193] Brown, Lester. *The Great Food Crisis of 2011.* Foreign Policy Magazine, Retrieved June 21, 2012.

[194] Ayres, E. *Will We Still Eat Meat?* Time Magazine, Nov 8, 1999. Vol 154 Issue 19 pg 107.

[195] United Nations Food and Agriculture Organization. *Livestock's Long Shadow. Environmental Issues and Options.* 2006, Pg 167.

[196] United Nations Food and Agriculture Organization. *Livestock's Long Shadow. Environmental Issues and Options.* 2006, Pg 126.

[197] United Nations Food and Agriculture Organization. *Livestock's Long Shadow. Environmental Issues and Options.* 2006, Pg 72.

[198] Robbins, J. *The Food Revolution.* San Francisco, CA. Conari Press 2001. Pg 234.

[199] Sierra Club of Iowa. http://iowa.sierraclub.org/Manure%20Spills%20and%20Fish%20Kills.pdf. Retrieved June 21, 2012.

[200] Robbins, J. *The Food Revolution.* San Francisco, CA. Conari Press 2001. Pg 242.

[201] Ebert, T. *The Dangerous Truth: Why Eating Meat is Ruining Your Health and Destroying the Environment.* Pg. 19.

[202] United Nations Food and Agriculture Organization. *Livestock's Long Shadow. Environmental Issues and Options.* 2006, Pg 137.

[203] United Nations Food and Agriculture Organization. *Livestock's Long Shadow. Environmental Issues and Options.* 2006, Pg 139.

[204] United Nations Food and Agriculture Organization. *Livestock's Long Shadow. Environmental Issues and Options.* 2006, Pg 156.

[205] Bittman M. *Rethinking the Meat Guzzler.* New York Times, Week in Review; January 27, 2008.

[206] Ebert, T. *The Dangerous Truth: Why Eating Meat is Ruining Your Health and Destroying the Environment.* Pg. 20.

[207] Burkholder, *Insidious Effects of Toxic Estaurine Dinoflagellate*; Burkholder, JM, *Pfiesteria Piscicida and Other Toxic Pfiesteria-Like Dinoflagellates,* North Carolina State University 1997; Chesapeake Bay Foundation, *Facts About Pfiesteria Piscicida.*

[208] Letson, David, and Gjollehon, Noel. *"Confined Animal Production and the Manure Problem."* Choices. (3rd Quarter 1996) Pg. 18.

[209] Cone M. *"State Dairy Farms Try to Clean Up Their Act."* Los Angeles Times, 28 April 1998. http://articles.latimes.com/1998/apr/28/news/mn-43842 Retrieved 10 Nov 2012.

[210] United Nations Food and Agriculture Organization. *Livestock's Long Shadow. Environmental Issues and Options.* 2006, Pg 142.

[211] United Nations Food and Agriculture Organization. *Livestock's Long Shadow. Environmental Issues and Options.* 2006, Pg 71.

[212] United Nations Food and Agriculture Organization. *Livestock's Long Shadow. Environmental Issues and Options.* 2006, Pg xxii.

[213] United Nations Food and Agriculture Organization. *Livestock's Long Shadow. Environmental Issues and Options.* 2006, Pg 32.

[214] United Nations Food and Agriculture Organization. *Livestock's Long Shadow. Environmental Issues and Options.* 2006, Pg 48.

[215] United Nations Food and Agriculture Organization. *Livestock's Long Shadow. Environmental Issues and Options.* 2006, Pg 162.

[216] United Nations Food and Agriculture Organization. *Livestock's Long Shadow. Environmental Issues and Options.* 2006, Pg 73.

[217] United Nations Food and Agriculture Organization. *Livestock's Long Shadow. Environmental Issues and Options.* 2006, Pg 64.

[218] United Nations Food and Agriculture Organization. *Livestock's Long Shadow. Environmental Issues and Options.* 2006, Pg 66.

[219] United Nations Food and Agriculture Organization. *Livestock's Long Shadow. Environmental Issues and Options.* 2006, Pg 76.

[220] http://www.hsph.harvard.edu/nutritionsource/what-should-you-eat/calcium-full-story. Retrieved March 2012.

[221] Vogiatzoglou A, Refsum H, Johnston C, et al. (2008). *Vitamin B_{12} status and rate of brain volume loss in community-dwelling elderly.* Neurology 71 (11): 826–32.

[222] Walsh, Stephen, RD. *Vegan Society B_{12} Factsheet.* Vegan Society. Retrieved 2008-01-17.

[223] Donaldson, MS (2000). *Metabolic vitamin B_{12} status on a mostly raw vegan diet with follow-up using tablets, nutritional yeast, or probiotic supplements.* Ann Nutr Metab 44 (5–6): 229–234.